This Railway Atlas of Great Britain and Ireland has been published as a tribute to the work of George Bradshaw Cartographer, Surveyor, Publisher, Engraver, Copperplate and Lithographic Printer.

CRAMPTON LOCOMOTIVE "COURIER" 1850

First published 2012

© Paul Leslie Line, 2012

Text © Paul Leslie Line

Maps and Photographs © as per credits on page 144.

Printed in the West Midlands

British Library Cataloguing in Publication Data.
A catalogue record for this book is available from the British Library.

ISBN 9781844917907

Typesetting and origination by Kimberley-Jane Turrell

Historical maps available to buy at
www.mapseeker.co.uk

Centaur Steam Engine from the Grand Junction Railway 1838

ARMCHAIR TIME TRAVELLERS
RAILWAY ATLAS

BRADSHAWS RAILWAY ATLAS
GREAT BRITAIN AND IRELAND - 1852

MAPSEEKER ARCHIVE PUBLISHING

FOREWORD BY VIC BRADSHAW-MITCHELL

ILLUSTRATED BY KIMBERLEY-JANE TURRELL

FOREWORD

I am thrilled to find this historic map produced as a manageable atlas, devoid of tubes or folds. It will bring joy to others with a passion for maps, doubly so if they are among those who enjoy railways, Britain's second biggest hobby.

It complements our own large series of railway albums, which have a detailed map of every station illustrated. Reviewers have said that we are "evolving the ultimate rail encyclopaedia" and this atlas is a must for those who enjoy a visual representation of history, rather than pages of dry text.

I enthuse about Bradshaw's products and did so on BBC Radio 4, this revealing many other such admirers. BBC TV has generated even greater interest by the frequent presentation of "Bradshaw's Guide". Having reprinted the 1866 edition profusely, it will delight many to find its relevant page numbers are shown herein.

My pen name came into use in 2007, when I began publishing "Railtimes for Great Britain" twice a year. I did not expect to promote Bradshaw's name in a Foreword as well!

Vic Bradshaw-Mitchell

The Offices of Bradshaw and Blacklock at 27, Brown Street, Manchester. and known back in the day as: "The House of Bradshaw"

ACKNOWLEDGEMENTS

This atlas, dedicated to George Bradshaw, has only been made possible as a result of many hours of passionate and meticulous work by those who were enthused by the idea of its creation. I would like to express my grateful thanks and acknowledgments to everyone who has played a part in this tribute to a man who, until recently, was unknown to many. It's now fitting that, thanks to their efforts, George Bradshaw's legacy to the nation is now also a visual gateway to the days when railway travel was at the height of Victorian eminence.

Steve Toulouse, Senior Graphic Artist at Mapseeker Publishing, for his painstaking work in recreating George Bradshaw's Railway Map of Great Britain and Ireland 1852 from the antique original, and Paul Lloyd for kindly sourcing it. Kimberley Jane for her illustrative skills in the visual representation and compilation.

Matthew Langham for his splendid introduction and editorial work throughout the Atlas; Phil Bradney for his tireless work in research and editing of the index of Railway Stations, Carla Johnston for additional research, Gary Byatt for his excellent IT support services.

Vic Bradshaw-Mitchell for the valuable publishing collaboration with the Middleton Press and their recent publication of Bradshaw's Guide (ISBN 9781908174055)

Lynn Hughes for her wonderful pencil and charcoal drawing of George Bradshaw, taken from an antique print sourced by Arthur Hook.

Paul Leslie Line

THE AVON VIADUCT NEAR RUGBY

INTRODUCTION

It is difficult to understate just how far reaching an impact the Age of Steam had on Victorian society, even given the benefit of 150 years of hindsight. The first public steam railway was opened in 1825, running between Darlington and Stockton on Tees in northeast England, with the world's first intercity railway, the Liverpool - Manchester Railway, following shortly after in 1830. Britain not only innovated in this field but also literally set the standard – the international standard gauge track width of 1,435mm was adopted from early British rail and was used in over half the world's railways. A mere 20 years on from its introduction, the railways had exploded - by the early 1850s Britain had over 7,000 miles of railway track, an amount which still dwarfs that of motorway in use today.

It is easy, however, to understand just how and why rail travel in particular was so successful. An obvious boon to heavy industry during the later stages of the Industrial Revolution, it expanded haulage, fostered trade and provided jobs centred at railway engineering towns like Crewe, Middlesbrough and Peterborough. Crucially though, it also provided accessible and affordable transport for all, advancing the country from one that operated on a local level – most people previously unable to travel more than 15 miles from their homes - to a national one as journey times were slashed. London to Birmingham, which previously took 11 hours by horse-drawn stagecoach in the 1830's, took just 3 hours by rail in the 1850s. This lead to new associated industries springing up – tourism boomed at seaside resorts which expanded to cater for those now able to take day trips to the coast at places like Brighton, Blackpool and Scarborough. As postal services improved, news travelled faster, as did fresh foods. Such benefits – the beginnings of the sort of modern conveniences we now enjoy as standard - were felt by all sections of society across a country which became easily interconnected on a practical level for the first time. The railway was truly egalitarian, its benefits not discriminating on class terms – women became more independent and the working classes geographically liberated almost at a stroke.

It was in this spirit that George Bradshaw, a cartographer and publisher, came to be fascinated by the railways. He was born in 1801, fittingly in Salford, the heartland of the innovation in transport, and the introduction of the railway prompted his Bradshaw's Guide to first appear in 1839, a cloth bound handbook costing sixpence. He had begun travelling the country in an attempt to collate local rail timetables into a handy volume, a novel idea at the time, with his Guide distributed across the country for the benefit of the new traveller. However, matters evolved as Bradshaw – a Quaker and philanthropist - was as interested in the people and places connected by the railways as he was in the technology itself.

ASTON CHURCH AND VIADUCT - BIRMINGHAM

INTRODUCTION

As he travelled to collect the required information, his Guide took on a new dimension as a travelogue and forerunner to the tourist guide, vividly describing the character of the people and places he visited. Using language full of character, these were not always flattering – Merthyr Tydfil, for example, "is best seen by night, for by day it is a wretched place". Elsewhere he reflects the preoccupations of the age, one concerned with leisure and social standing – regarding Weymouth there was "No place (can be) more salubrious… the air is so pure and mild that the town is not only frequented during the summer but has been selected by many opulent families as a permanent residence." He was, though, still in thrall to technology and the wonder of human engineering operating then on an unprecedented scale, describing the new tunnels, viaducts and bridges that made the new-found feat of train travel possible.

Bradshaw's early cartographic work had started with his detailed plans showing the canals and navigable rivers, and with the arrival of steam powered travel his work coalesced into maps showing the extensive routes of the railway. This book reproduces a highly digitised version of his rare New Railway Map of Great Britain and Ireland of 1852, published just a year before his death. Art worked for the very first time and presented in glorious full colour, the exquisite map sections display the original Victorian railway routes, including some 1700 stations, in intricate detail across Britain, Ireland and northern France. This book has been designed specifically to dovetail perfectly with Bradshaw's Guide – station's are indexed to where they can be found in the atlas pages, if they are named in the Bradshaw's Guide then the relevant page number at the bottom of the Guide book is also recorded for that station therefore allowing the reader to actually follow any journey described in such vivid detail by the travel pioneer. In addition to this all 22 detailed British Town plans published by John Tallis in 1851, which contain beautifully drawn Victorian era city views from the period, are included and presented in full page spreads, allowing the reader to visualise both the plans and vistas of the central city hubs that the contemporary traveller would have arrived in following a journey on the railway ending in any major British or Irish city.

Just as the transport technology of Bradshaw's time enabled new travel experiences, modern sophisticated scanning and digital techniques have brought Bradshaw's map and the countless journeys documented in the Bradshaw's Guide back to life for the first time. It is hoped that Bradshaw's labour of love, in particular his magnificent cartographic creations as presented and commemorated in this atlas, will enable the reader to trace and relive the rich travel experiences of a country on the cusp of modern life in 1852.

Matthew Langham

THE RAILWAY STATION - CHESTER

"BRITANNIA" TUBULAR RAILWAY BRIDGE, ACROSS MENAI STRAITS, FROM THE ANGLESEY ABUTMENT 1849

CONTENTS

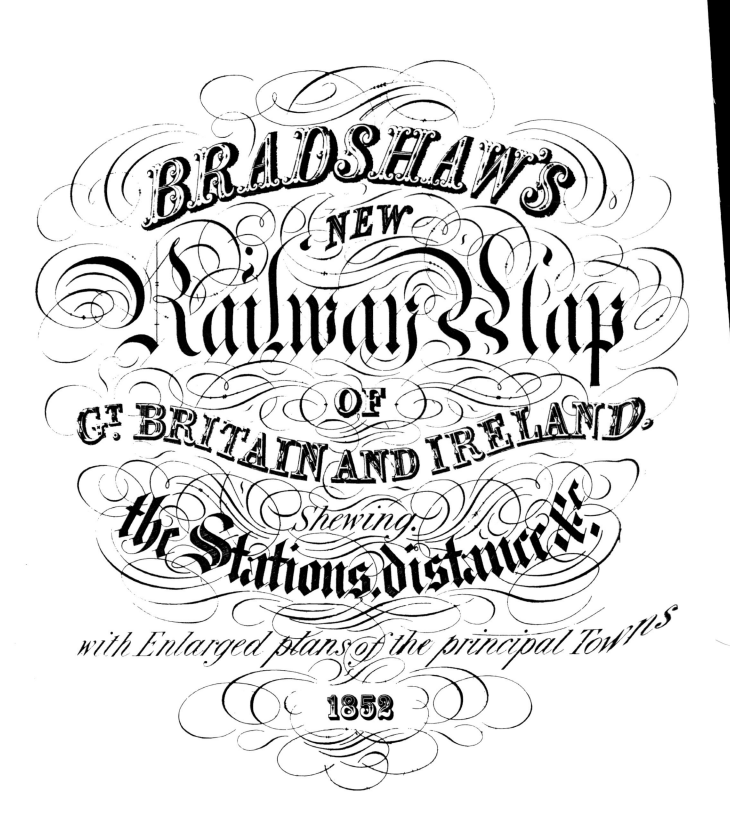

BRADSHAW'S NEW Railway Map OF GT. BRITAIN AND IRELAND, Shewing. the Stations, distance &c.

with Enlarged plans of the principal Towns

1852

One
BRADSHAW'S RAILWAY MAP OF GREAT
BRITAIN AND IRELAND 1852

This most informative and colourful railway map displays George Bradshaw's fine ability as a cartographer, his impeccable eye for detail and creativity without bounds which he installed into his publishing company, Bradshaw and Blacklock. Considering the rate at which railways were being constructed across Great Britain and Ireland, requiring the constant reassessment of information, it seems incredible that one detailing all the stations, along with distances between, was produced at the time. The original colours denoting the principal railway companies - faded on the original - have been maintained and enhanced, adding to this informative resource. The table below is an exact representation of that on the original folded sheet map.

Pages 12 and 13 show the full extent of the railway map covering Great Britain and Ireland, along with parts of France, and is the key page to the Atlas. The map allows the many railway routes to be followed, station by station, by following the "Go to" arrows in the page margins. Tracing these routes gives a nostalgic glimpse into the mid-nineteenth century, one deepened by the incorporation of many views and vistas, just as they would have been seen by the many first time travellers embarking on the great railway journeys at the height of railway mania. We have only added one textual description, that of the Great Dee Viaduct, which represents just one of many iconic feats of human ingenuity created in establishing the national railway network. It is lovingly and passionately described by someone, now sadly unknown, in the elegant, flowery style of a well-spoken Victorian person, just as the rest of the Railway Journeys are also described in Bradshaw's Railway Guide.

Aberdeen	Blue	South Eastern	Dark Red
Birkenhead, Lancashire & Chester Junction	Purple	South Staffordshire	Green
Caledonian	Crimson	Shrewsbury & Birmingham	Blue
Dundee and Pert	Yellow	South Devon	Red
Eastern Union	Orange	South Wales	Green
Eastern Counties	Blue	Scottish Midland	Orange
East Lancashire	Brown	Scottish Central	Green
East Anglian	Yellow	York Newcastle & Berwick	Pink
Edinburgh & Glasgow	Blue	York & North Midland	Dark Green
Edinburgh & Northern	Purple	Bristol & Exeter	Yellow
Glasgow & South Western	Brown	Midland	Yellow
Great Northern	Orange	North Western	Brown
Great Western -	Blue	North Staffordshire	Purple
London & North Western	Crimson	Newcastle and Carlisle	Yellow
Leeds & Thirsk	Brown	North British	Yellow
Lancaster and Carlisle	Green	Stockton & Darlington	Yellow
London & South Western	Orange	Shrewsbury & Chester	Yellow
Lancashire & Yorkshire	Blue	Stockton & Hartlepool	Purple
London Brighton & South Coast	Green	South Eastern	Dark Red
Manchester Sheffield and Lincolnshire	Light Green	South Staffordshire	Green
Midland	Yellow	Shrewsbury & Birmingham	Blue
North Western	Brown	South Devon	Red
North Staffordshire	Purple	South Wales	Green
Newcastle and Carlisle	Yellow	Scottish Midland	Orange
North British	Yellow	Scottish Central	Green
Stockton & Darlington	Yellow	York Newcastle & Berwick	Pink
Shrewsbury & Chester	Yellow	York & North Midland	Dark Green
Stockton & Hartlepool	Purple	Bristol & Exeter	Yellow

BRADSHAW'S RAILWAY MAP OF GREAT
BRITAIN AND IRELAND 1852

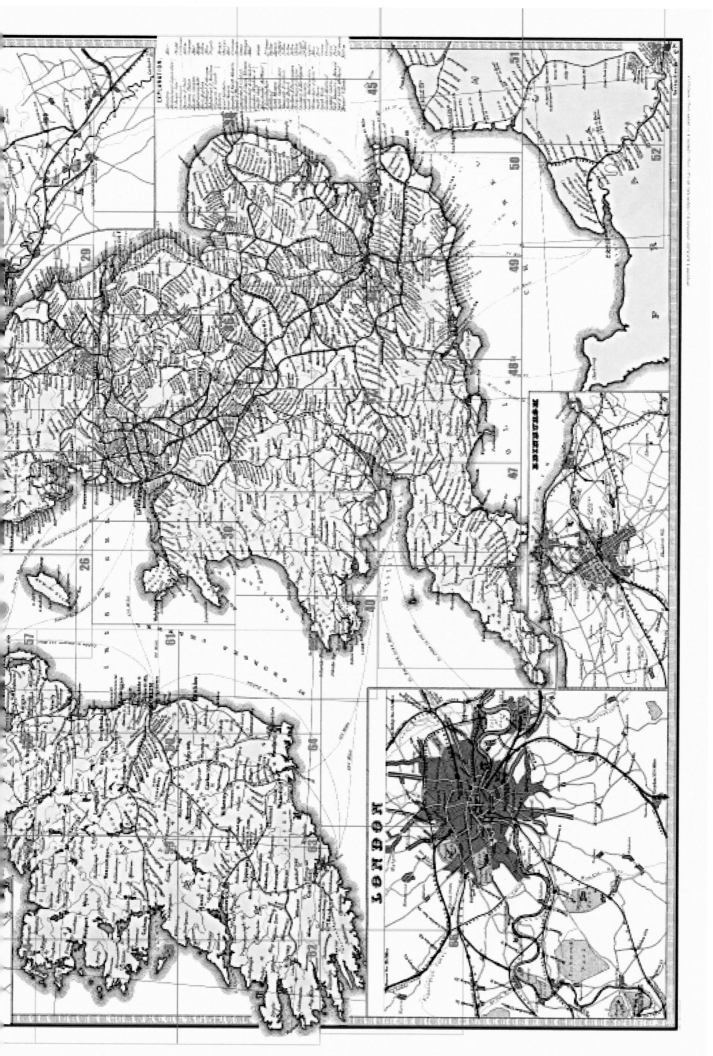

CLAN MCKENZIE

Frec...

Durness

Arolvore

Gleng

S

Stour H^d.

Loadmore

More H^d.

Kiergag

Kinloch A

PART OF

CROMARTY

Ardnote

New

Pollew

Loch Broom R

Storn

H

Gairloc

Callal..

Garowgan

S

Din

Applecross

S

Bea

Lochcarron

14

Go to page 19 ▽

Go to page 16 ▷

Go to page 20 ▽

INVERNESS

Go to page 15

BANFF IN THE COUNTY OF BANFFSHIRE 1836

DUNOLLY CASTLE - ARGYLESHIRE

GLENCOE

18

Go to page 22 ▽

Go to page 14

Applecross

Beauley

Inverr

Lochcarron

Do

Strane

Lochalsh

Urquha

Kintail

Strath

Fort Augustus H

Glenshiel

N

R

Sandwide

Balalista

I

N

Sourlies

V

E

Shanavell

Bellagluoy

Moy

Fort William

rnsam

Ardgower

Corrygrant

Sunart

Corriherich

Auti

Ulidill

Kinlochmore

Fo

Glencoe

E

Myanl

Appin

Inveroran

L

Killin

Bunaw

Loc

Oban

Glenorchy Balquhidder

Kilchrennan

CALLANDER

Kilmorich

INVERARY

Ardgartan

bridge of

Strachur

S

Go to page 20

Go to page 23

Go to page 14

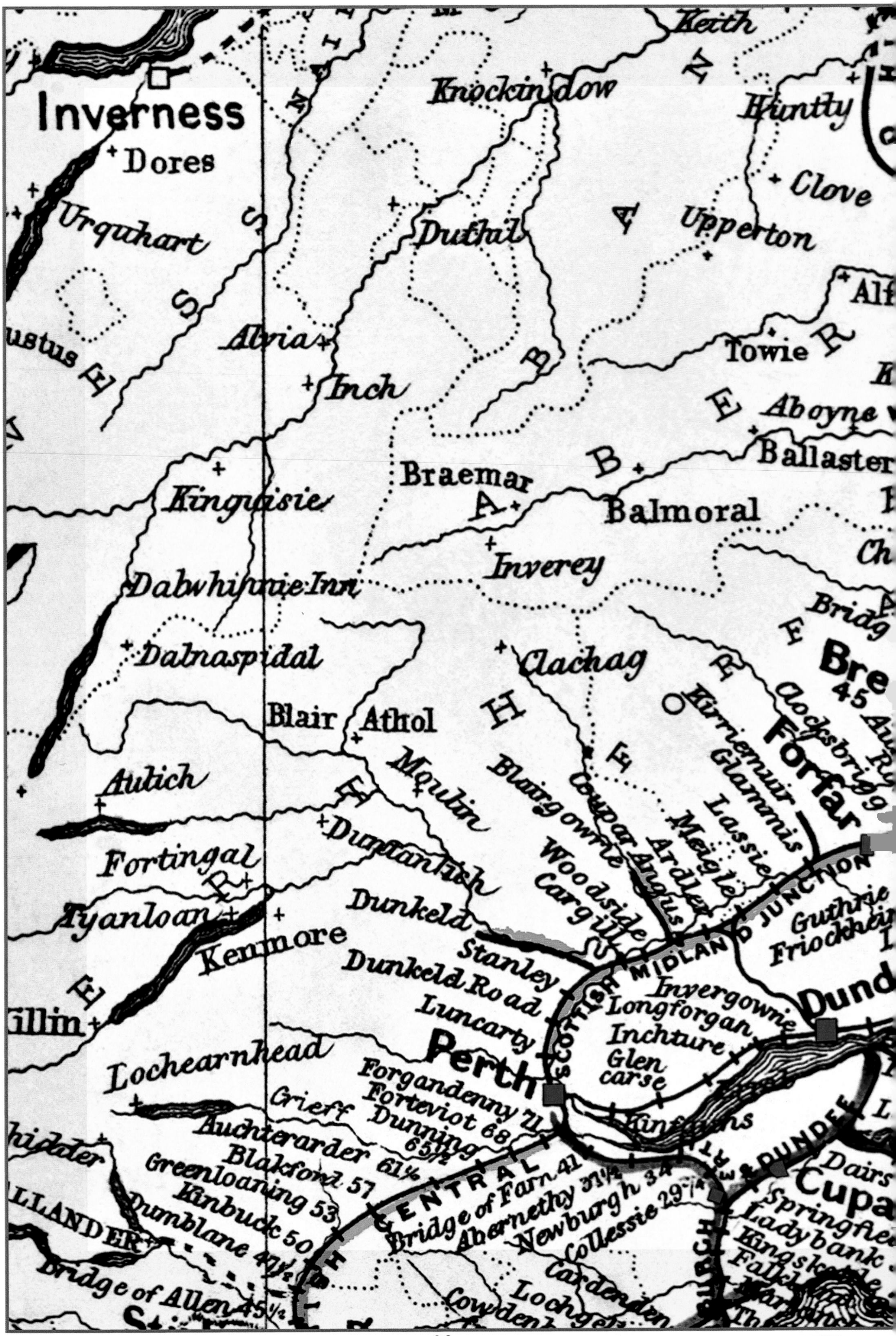

Inverness
+Dores

Urquhart

Knockindow

Huntly

Clove

Duthil

Upperton

+Alf

Towie

R

E

Aboyne

Abria +

Inch

Braemar

B

Ballaster

Kinguisie

A

Balmoral

Ch

+ Inverey

Dalwhinnie Inn

Bridg

Dalnaspidal

Clachag

Bre

45 Au

H

Forfar

Aultich

Moulin

Blair Athol

Blairgowrie

Kirriemuir

Cocksbrigg

Glammis

Lassie

Fortingal

Duptanlich

Woodside

Cargill

Coupar Angus

Ardler

Meagle

Guthrie

Friockhei

R

Ayanloan

Dunkeld

Stanley

SCOTCH MIDLAND JUNCTION

Invergownie

Longforgan

Dund

Kenmore

Dunkeld Road

Luncarty

Inchture

Glen carse

illin

Lochearnhead

Perth

Kin ons

DUNDEE

Forgandenny

Forteviot 68

Dunning 65½

Longforgan

Dairs

Cupa

Crieff

Auchterarder 61½

Blakford 57

Greenloaning 53

Kinbuck 50

Dumblane 47½

CENTRAL

Bridge of Farn 41

Abernethy 31½

Newburgh 34

Collessie 29¼

Springfe

Ladybank

Kingsker

Falc

hidder

LLANDER

Bridge of Allen 45½

S

Cowden

Lochgels

Carden den

Go to page 19

Go to page 24

Go to page 15 △

New Deer
Tarves
Old Meldrum
SCOTLAND
Kintore
Peterhead
Newburgh
Black Dog
Aberdeen
O'Niel
cardine
Durris
nchory
KINCARDINE
Edinb.
Glasg.
Cove 4½
Portlethen 7½
Muchalls 10¾
Crippet Mill
Stonehaven 15¾
Drumlithie 22¾
Fordoun 26¾
Laurencekirk 30¼
Mark ark 34¼
Dubton Junction 38¾
Montrose 41 ¾
fr. Aberdeen
44½
Arbroath 57
fr. Aberdeen
East Haven
Carnoustie
Barnheth
Broughty Ferry 45
Port on Craig 44
chars Junc.n 39
St Andrews
35½
32
30
f Dun Junc.
hin
f Drun
nc.
Junc.
gsmill
Colliston
Farnell R.
Firth of Forth

BRACKLIN BRIDGE

PERTH

21

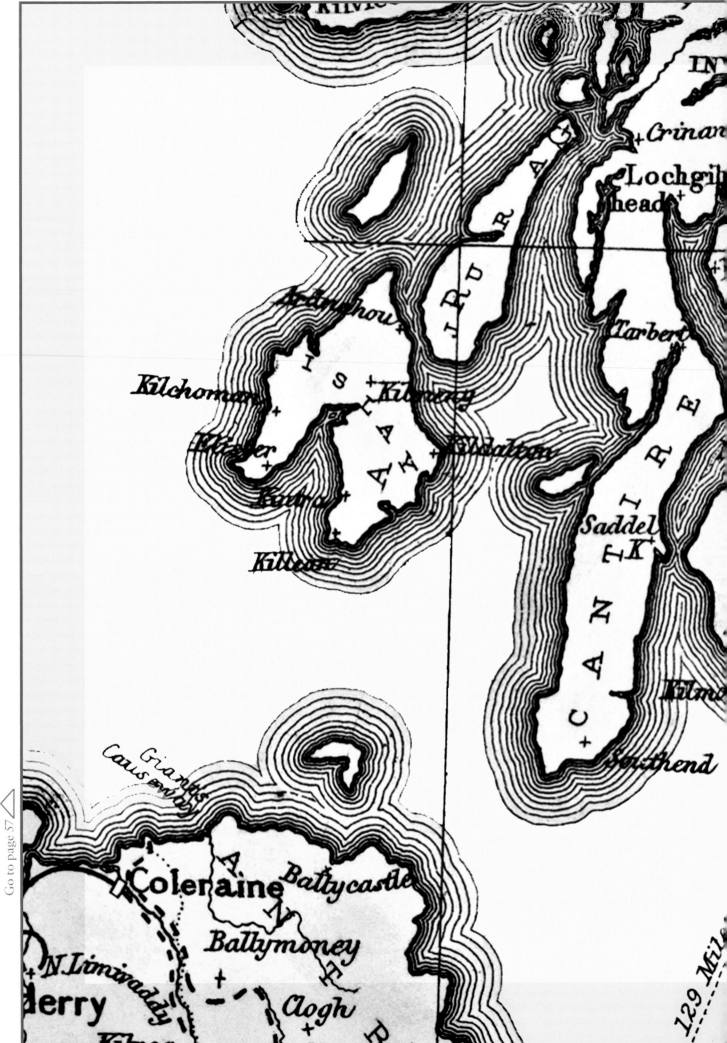

Go to page 57

Kilmorich

ERARY

Ardgartan

Strachur

Kilmodan

finnan

Helensburgh

68¾

Greenock

Port Glasgow

Johnstone 10

Shrane Mill 11½

innoch 13¾

eith 17¾

nnie 19¾

ry 20½

winnig 26

Androssan

Saltcoat

Irvine 29

Dreghorn

Troon 34

Monkton 3

Prestwick 37

Ayr 40

Girvan

Dalmellington

Cairn

Ballintrae

Kirkcolme

Loch Lomond

Luss

Callander

Bridge of Allen 45½

Dumblane 49½

Kinbuck 50

Doaning 57

STIRLING

Stirling

Bannockburn 39½

Larbert 34

Greenhill Junc. 30

Scot. Central Junc.

Castle Cary 32

Campsie

nox own 11½

R. Kirkintilloch

Campsie Junc. 40¾

Miltown

Croy 36

Dunf

Dunfe

EDINBURGH

GLASGOW & GLA

SLAMANNA

Bathgat

Airdrie

Whifflet 11

Holytown 14

Motherwell

Shotts

Bishop ton

Paisley 7

Renfrew 7

402

GLASGOW

Neilston

Barrhead

Hamilton

Wishaw

Busby 35

Kilmarnock 37

Newmilns

Carluke 19

Lanark 25

Hurlford

Galston 42½

Mauchline 46½

Braidwood 20

Carstairs Junc.

Fall of the Clyde 27½

Thankerton 31½

Symington 33

Lamington 37

Abington 42

Auchinleck

Cumnock

GLASGOW SOUTH

Muirkirk

Sanquhar

Thornhill

Closeburn

Dumfries

Carsphairn

Dalry

New Galloway

Dee Bridge

Newton St

23

Go to page 24

Go to page 27

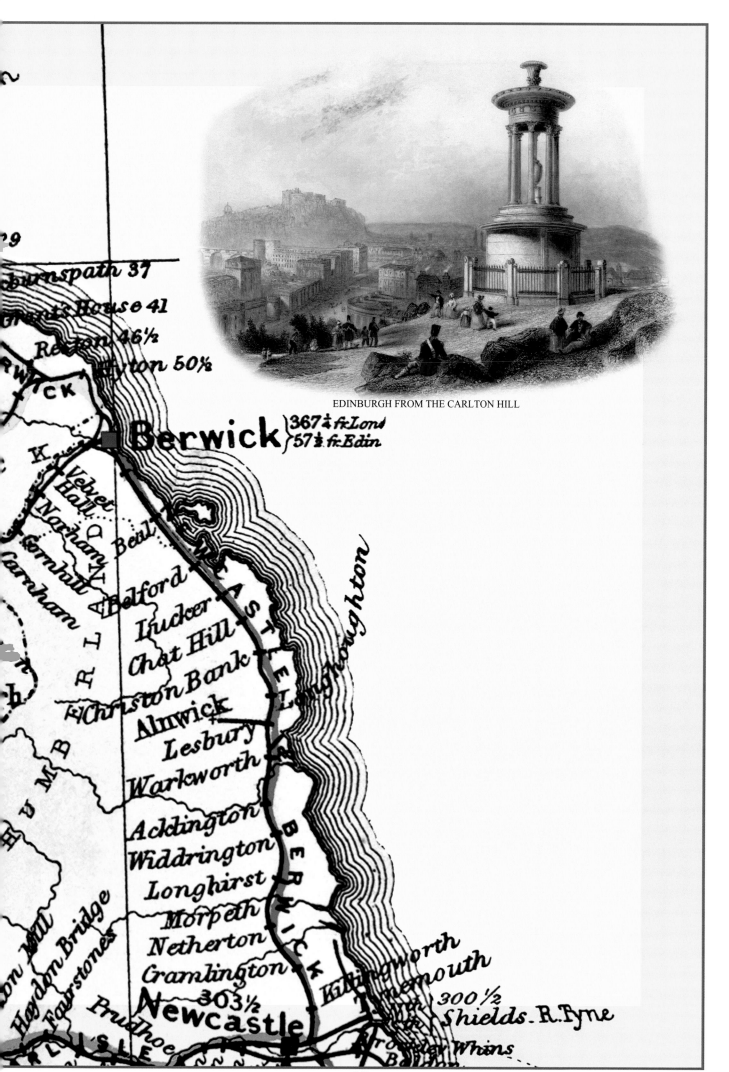

EDINBURGH FROM THE CARLTON HILL

ournspath 37
ound's House 41
Reston 46½
...rton 50½

...CK

Berwick }367¼ fr.Lond
57½ fr.Edin

NEWCASTLE

Velvet Hall
Nacham
...ornhill
Carrham
Belford
Beal
Lucker
Chat Hill
Christon Bank
Alnwick
Lesbury
Warkworth
Acklington
Widdrington
Longhirst
Morpeth
Netherton
Cramlington
Longhoughton
BERWICK
...on Hill
Haydon Bridge
Fourstones
Prudhoe
CARLISLE
Newcastle 303½
King...worth
...mouth
Shields R.Tyne
300½
...Whins
Bo...

NORTHUMBERLAND

25

Go to page 28 ▽

Go to page 23 △

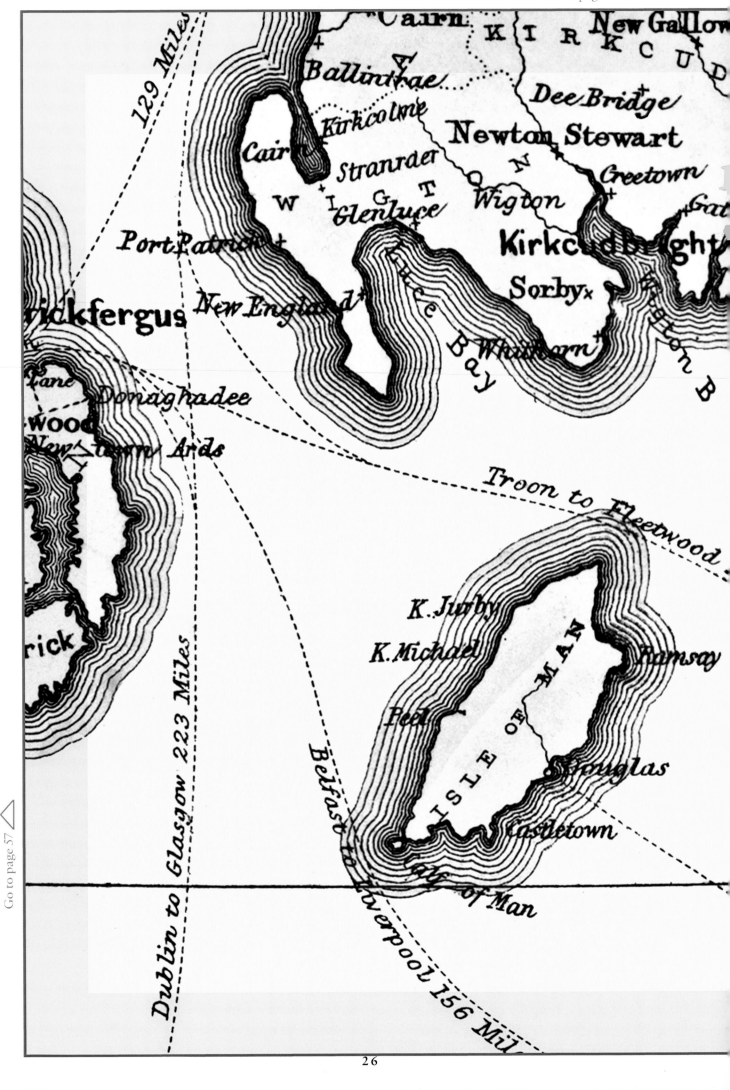

Go to page 57 ◁

Dumfries

CARLISLE

Ecclef... Kirtlebr... Kirkpatrick

Gretna Junc.

Scotby Wetherall How Hill Milton Low Row Rose Hill Greenhe... Hal...

Carlisle

NEWCASTLE

Dalston Knares...

Gurthwaite

Wigton

Leegate

Brisco

D Kirk...

Als...

Clayton Dalston

Arkleby

Southwaite

LANCASTER

Ball... re

Dearham

Plumpton

Maryport

Flimby

Cockermouth

Penrith

APP...

Workington

Brigham Cam... Broughton

Penrith

Clifton

R I...

Harrington Parton

Workington Bee

Rossthwaite

KENDAL

WEST

M

+

Whitehaven

Egremont

Shap

Kirb...

St Bee

B

WEST

Netherton

Braysto...

Sellafield

Seascale

WHITEHAVEN & FURNESS

Tebay

Drig

Winander

Ravengla...

Mere

Staveley

Burneside

Low G...

Eskmeal...

Broughton

Kirkby

Kendal

Se...

Boot...

FURNESS

Milnthorpe

Kendal Junc.

Silecroft

CARLISLE

Holborn Hill

Ulverston Burton

Dalton Carnforth

Walu...

FURNESS Abbey

Bolton

Hatton Hornby

Barrow

West Bord...

Island

Ramside

230

Lancaster

Go to page 28 ▷

25 Miles

Glasgow to Liverpool 250 Miles

75 Miles

Fleetwood

Gatgate

Bay Horse

Scorton

Garstang

Brock

Brough -ton

Blackpool

Kirkham

Salwick

Lea Rd

Poulton

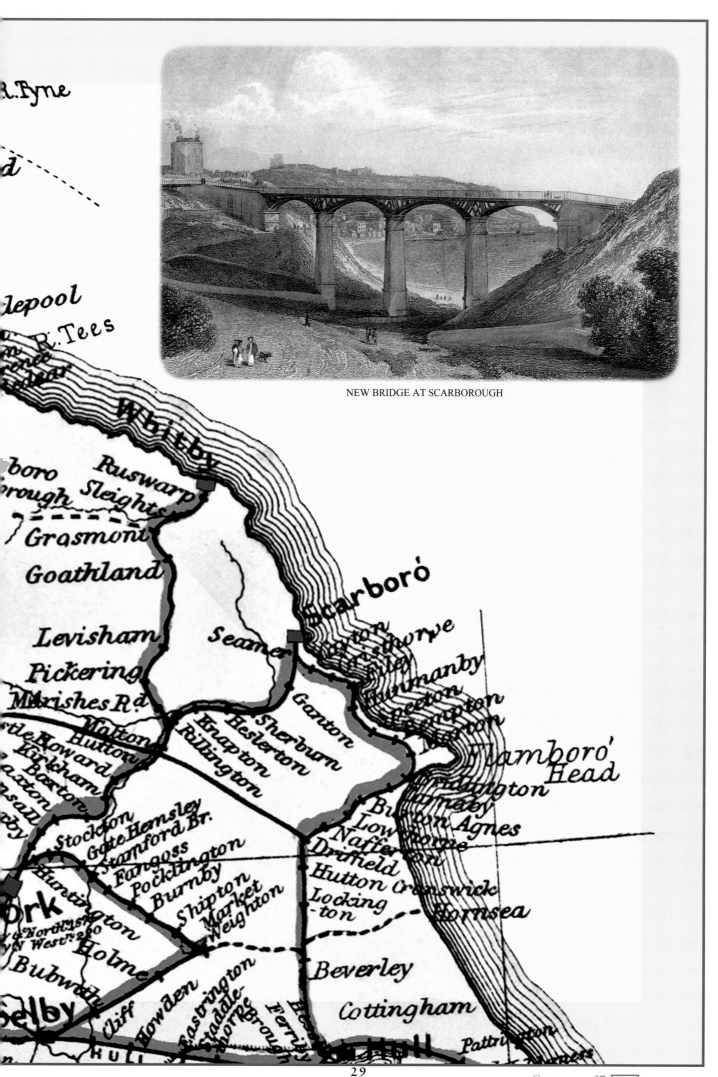

NEW BRIDGE AT SCARBOROUGH

29

Go to page 37 ▽

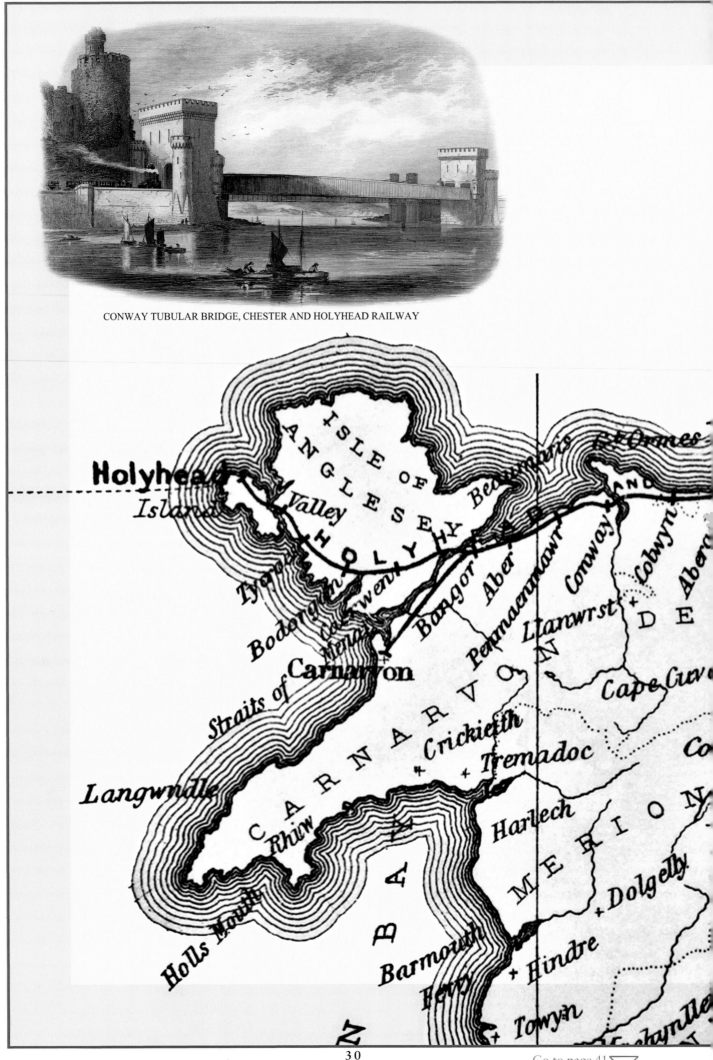

CONWAY TUBULAR BRIDGE, CHESTER AND HOLYHEAD RAILWAY

Go to page 41

Go to page 27 △

Go to page 36 ▷

Go to page 42 ▽

CONWAY STATION

OGWEN VIADUCT

BANGOR STATION

VIEW OF BANGOR, 1852 "THE ATHENS OF WALES"

THE GREAT DEE VIADUCT ON THE SHREWSBURY TO CHESTER RAILWAY

By this noble structure, the Shrewsbury and Chester Railway crosses the river Dee, in the Vale of Llangollen, at one of the loveliest spots in the principality of Wales, where nature has grouped the various elements of beauty in the richest profusion, and art has recorded its triumphs by first class works. The view from the top of the Viaduct for extent and beauty is unequalled. Beneath winds the Dee, rushing by successive streams from pool to pool, glancing with silvery light o'er its pebbly channel in one spot, then loosing itself behind a steep bank covered with noble trees, and again appearing clam and tranquil in a glossy pool, in which are mirrored the overhanging banks in all the brilliant colours of a autumnal landscape.

From the winding river the Trevor Hills rise with serrated outline on the left bank, and the mountains forming the continuation of the Berwyn range abut on the right bank: their lower slopes are richly cultivated, and on successive terraces are dotted the white cottages of the Welsh peasantry, whilst masses of dark wood crown the projecting heights. The Aqueduct of Pontcysyllte, one of Telford's greatest works, is seen crossing the valley about a mile distant from the Viaduct, and forms a striking feature in the prospect.

The Castle Dinas Bran, the Barber's Hill, and the Glucig Rocks, form a background unrivalled for the picturesque effect and enclose the vale in an amphitheatre of loveliness. Railways, canals, lime quarries, and the distant iron-works mark the progress of commercial enterprise.

The stupendous Viaduct consists of 19 semicircular arches of 60 feet span; and the height from the bed of the river to the top of the parapet at the centre pier is 148 feet. Its length is 1532 feet. The arches are built with a double ring of arch stones four feet deep, having a broad chamfer cut off each arris; this double chamfered ring being continued down the piers without break to the foundation. There is no projecting or springing course to break the simple and majestic outline of the arch and piers.

The piers are thirteen feet thick, and twenty-eight feet six inches long at the springing of the arch; and have a curvilinear batten or slope on the face, which gives strength and graceful form to the whole. The Viaduct is founded on the solid rock, and is built of stone, with the exception of the interior arching, which is of hard fire bricks. The tint of the stone is warm and beautiful; the quoins or outer rings of the arches and piers are smoothly dressed; all the rest of the work is rough rustic, which conveys to the mind the idea of great strength and solidity. The parapet is set on a bold projecting string-course, supported on dentals, these parts are in single stones smoothly dressed, and give a noble finish to this portion of the design.

The first stone of this great work was laid on the 19th of April, 1846; and the last arch was closed on the 12th of August, 1848; but the ceremony of keying the last arch did not take place until the 25th of August. The construction thus occupied a period of two years and 4 months. The structure contains upwards of 64,000 cubic yards of solid masonry, and cost about £76,000. It is the largest of its class in the World yet erected in this country. This vast structure has been quietly and steadily completed without attracting public attention, it being scarcely known beyond the vale which it spans.

The Viaduct has been erected under the direction, and from the design of, Mr. Henry Robertson, the engineer of the Shrewsbury and Chester Railway, who originally laid out this portion of the Railway in November, 1845, and who has now conducted the works to successful completion.

The line was opened to the public on the 14th of this month. It connects the mineral districts of North Wales with the manufacturing districts, and forms an improved communication between the estuaries of the Dee and Bristol Channel. Birkenhead may be looked upon as its main goods terminus. Throughout its whole length from Chester to Shrewsbury, it traverses one of the richest portions of England, skirting the base of the welsh mountains.

THE GREAT DEE VIADUCT, 1851

Go to page 28 △

Go to page 31 ◁

Go to page 42 ▽

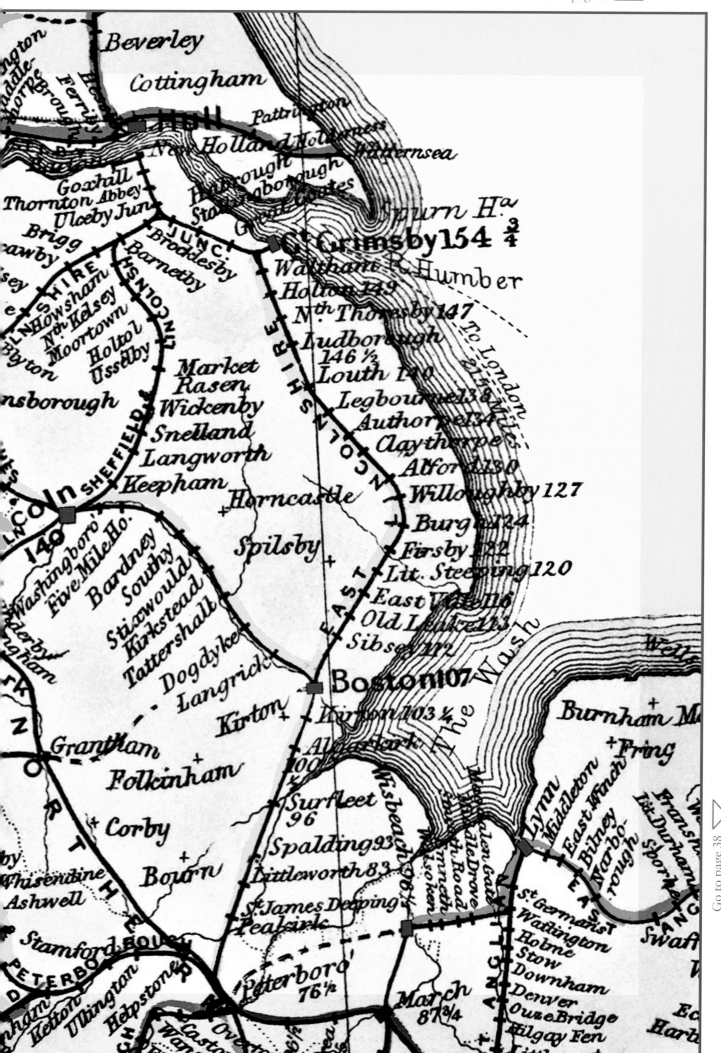

Beverley

Cottingham

Pattrington

N. Holland Holderness
... Withernsea

Goxhill
Thornton Abbey
Ulceby Junc.

Hull... borough Stocks... Coates

Brigg
Crawby

SHIRE
Howsham
Nth Kelsey
Moortown
Holton
Usselby
Blyton

LINCOLN JUNC.

Barnetby
Brocklesby
Junc.

Gt Grimsby 154 ¾

Waltham
Holton 149

Humber

Nth Thoresby 147

Ludborough
146½

Louth 140

Market
Rasen
Wickenby
Snelland
Langworth
Keepham

Legbourne 138

Authorpe 134

Claythorpes

Alford 130

Willoughby 127

Horncastle

Spilsby

Burgh 124

Firsby 122

Lit. Steeping 120

East Ville 116

Old Leake 113

Sibsey 112

To London 154 Miles

sborough

Lincoln
146

Washingboro
Five Mile Ho.
Bardney
Southy
Stixwould
Kirkstead
Tattershall

Dogdyke

Langrick

Kirton

Boston 107

Kirton 103¼

SHEFFIELD

EAST

The Wash

Burnham M
Fring

Grantham
Folkingham

Surfleet
96

Spalding 93

Littleworth 83

Lynn
Middleton
Bilney
East Winch
Narborough
Sporle

Corby
Bourn

Whisendine
Ashwell

St James Deeping
Peakirk

Stamford BOURN

PETERBORO

Uffington
Helpstone

Peterboro
76½

March
87¾

Walpole
Wisbeach
Gedney
... Drove
...

Lynn Gate
St Germans
Watlington
Holme
Stow
Downham
Denver
Ouze Bridge
Tilgay Fen

Swaff

NORTH

EAST ANG

37

Go to page 38 ▷

NORWICH CASTLE

Go to page 37

Go to page 45

YARMOUTH, WITH NELSONS'S MONUMENT c1840

ABERYSTWYTH

Holls M...

CARD...

Or...

Cardigan

Strumble H.   Newport

Abermaw   Fishguard

St. Davids Head   St. Davids   PEMBROK...

St. Brides Bay

Nalton

Haverfordwest

Milford   Neyland   Laug...

St. Anns Head

Pembrook   Pembrook

Linney Head

B...

les

40

Go to page 30

GAN B

Barmouth

Ferry + Hindre

Towyn

Machynlleth

MONTGOMERY

Wolshpool

Bishops Castle

R. Dovey or Dyfi

Llanidlos

Newtown

Aberystwith

Kinghton

RADNOR

Dryffryn

Aberafrom

Rhatador

Tregaron

Builth

CARDIG

+ Benbryn

Cwm Ann

Hay

Newcastle Emlyn

Methyr Cynog

Talgar

CARMARTHEN

narthwyd

Llandovery

Brecon

+ A

Carmarthen

Llangadock

BRECON

Llandilovawr

Abergau

Merthyr

ame

Kidwelly

VALE

Po

Swansey

Aberdare

Neath

Newbridge

SOUTH

Tenby to Bristol 115 Miles

Port Talbot

Bridgend

Llantrissant

Landaff

Cardiff

ris

41

Go to page 42

Go to page 47

Go to page 44

Go to page 49

Go to page 43

Go to page 50

NORWICH
BURY & NORWICH
Swainsthorpe
Flordon 106
Forncett 103½
Tivetshall 100
Burston 97
Diss 94½
Mellis 91
Finningham 86½
Haughley Junct? 81½
Stow Market 80
Needham 76¾
Claydon 73
Bramford 70¾
Ipswich
Bentley Junc 62½
Ardleigh
Colchester

Haddiscoe 141
Somerleyton 141⅜
Muxford 147¾
Leicester
Lowestoff

Halesworth
Framlingham
Alborough

To Yarmouth
M.
To Newcastle
Miles. To Newcastle
To Edinburgh

Harwich
Gravesend
Margate 101 Miles
North Foreland
Ramsgate 97 Ms
Sandwich 98

136 Miles
108

45

Redruth + Truro

Hayle

Marazion
Penzance

Penryn + Falmouth

+ Helston

End

C O R

B r i s t

To India 12,330 Miles

Lundy I.

Hartland +

Torr

Stratton +

Holswort

D

Launceston +

More

Padst

Camelford

L

Tavistock

Plymouth

Devonport

C

O

R

N

W

A

L

L

Podmin +

Liskeard

Lostwithiel +

St Austell +

St Gem

Redruth + Truro

Hayle

Pen

Go to page 40

Go to page 48

Go to page 47

Go to page 43

Go to page 50

HUNGERFORD BRANCH

Gori... 44

52¾

...chatcham

Woolhampton

Aldermaston

Basingstoke 48¼

Theale 41

JUNCTION

Mortimer

Winchfield 40

Fleetpond 37½

Farnborough 33

READING

WESTER

Windsor 21

Wokingham

Datchet

Blackw.ᵗ

Staines 19¼

Chertsey

Woking 33

Woking 25

GUILDFORD

Houns...

Trays...

bury

Ashf...

Feltham 15

Weybridge 19¼

Walton 17

Esher 15

Epsom 18½

Ewell

Cheam

Sutton

Morsham 19

New...

Rich mond 10

Croydon 11

Woolw...

Abb...

Charlton 8

Gross...

BRIGHTON

Reigate Junc. 21

Godst... 27

Whitchurch

Andover Road 58

Alton 1...

Farnham 48

Ash 48

Farnham

Guildford

Godalming

Shalford 40

Chilworth 38

Sheire Heath 35

Gomshall 34

Dorking 34

Black.w.ᵗ 28

Box Hill 28

Reigate 23

Reigate

Crawley

Fay Gate 34

Horsham 37¾

Horley 25

3 Bridges 1...

Eas...

Grin...

Balcombe

Havkar...

Heath 3...

Winchester 67

Petersfield...

Bishopstoke Junc

Porchester 88

Cosham 88

Havant 88

Emsworth 86

Bosham 82

SOUTH COAST

Burgess Hill 41½

Hassocks Gate 43½

Kingstone

Lancing

Hove

LONDON

Fah...

Isle of Wight

Portsmouth 94

Chi...

Drayton...

Boston 77

Y... 74

Chichel 71½

...thampton 68½

...thering 66

...shing 63¾

...ring 61

...eham 56½

Bognock

Brighton

102 Miles

94 Miles

N

T

S

S

U

S

S

O

C

H

49

Go to page 43

Go to page 49

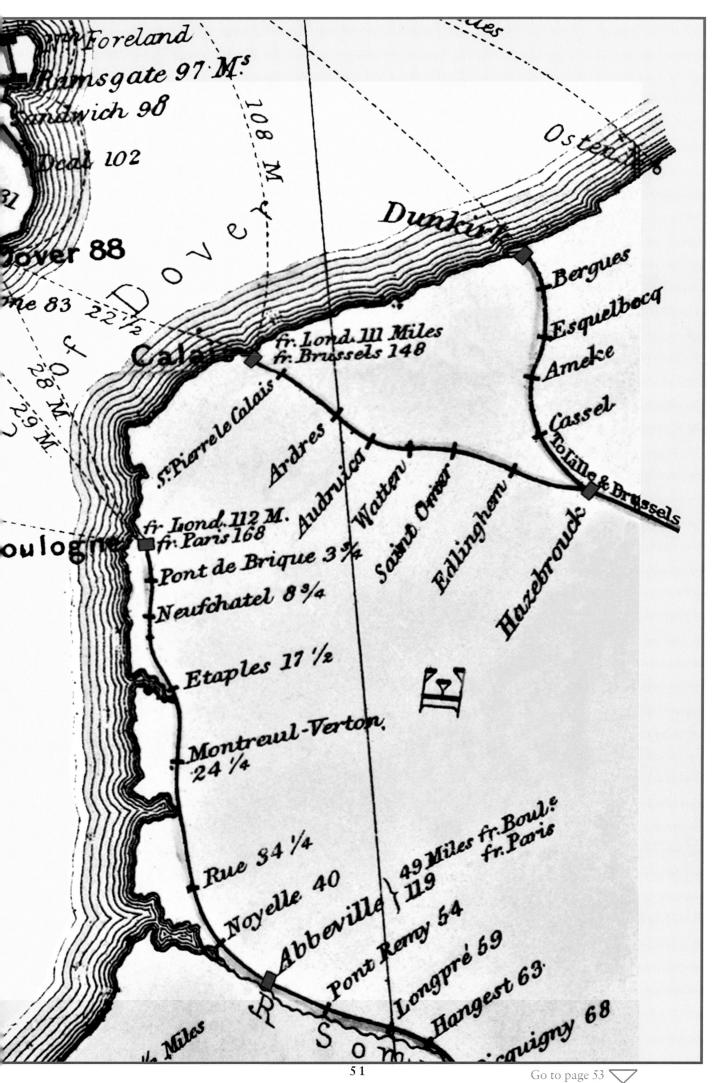

Foreland

Ramsgate 97 M.ˢ

andwich 98

Deal 102

37

Dover 88

one 83   22½

28 M.

29 M.

Dover

Gulf of

Calais

fr. Lond. 111 Miles
fr. Brussels 148

Dunkirk

Osten

Bergues

Esquelbocq

Ameke

Cassel

To Lille & Brussels

St Pierre le Calais

Ardres

Audruica

Watten

Saint Omer

Edlinghem

Hazebrouck

E

oulogne

fr. Lond. 112 M.
fr. Paris 168

Pont de Brique 3¾

Neufchatel 8¾

Etaples 17½

Montreul-Verton.
24¼

Rue 34¼

Noyelle 40

Abbeville } 119

49 Miles fr. Boul.ᵉ
fr. Paris

Pont Remy 54

Longpré 69

Hangest 63

R

So

Miles

icquigny 68

51

Go to page 53 ▽

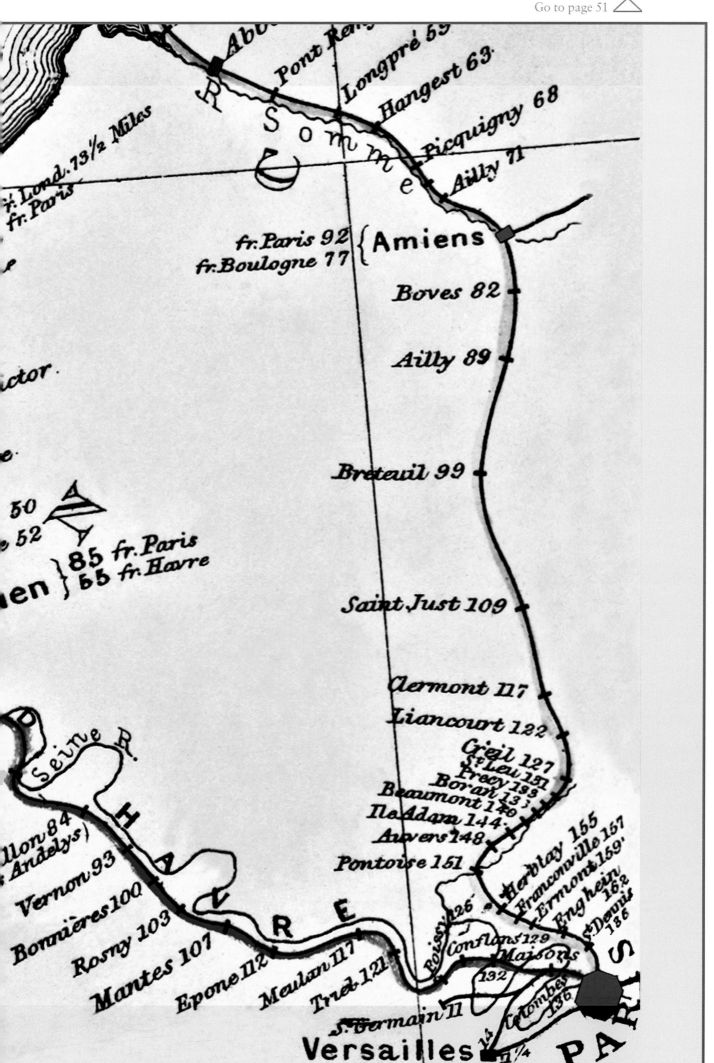

fr. Lond. 73½ Miles
fr. Paris

R⎬S O M M E

Abb
Pont Rem⸺
Longpré 59
Hangest 63
Picquigny 68
Ailly 71

fr. Paris 92 ⎱ **Amiens**
fr. Boulogne 77 ⎰

Boves 82

Ailly 89

Breteuil 99

Saint Just 109

Clermont 117

Liancourt 122

Creil 127
St Leu 131
Precy 133
Boran 136
Beaumont 140
Ile Adam 144
Auvers 148
Pontoise 151

Herblay 155
Franconville 167
Ermont 159
Enghein 162
St Denis 166

50
52

en ⎱ 85 fr. Paris
⎰ 55 fr. Havre

victor

Seine R.

H A V R E

llon 84
Andelys)
Vernon 93
Bonnières 100
Rosny 103
Mantes 107
Epone 112
Meulan 117
Triel 121
St Germain 11

26
Conflans 129
Maisons
132
Colombes
136

P A R I S

Versailles 11/4

53

Go to page 58 ▽

Malahide 9 Miles fr. Dub.

To Drogheda

DROGHEDA

arnock 6¾

nction 4¾

3¾

BLIN

Baldoyle & Sutton
7 Miles

Howth 8¼

HOWTH BR.CH

Hill of
Howth
563 feet

DUBLIN

Light Ho.

Harbour

Kight Ho.

Gortahor ×

× Dunglod

Nairen

Ardara ×

Killybergs

Donegal

KINGSTOWN

Blackrock 4¾ Y

Hill 5¼

stown
Miles

To Bray &
Wicklow

ATMOSPH.
LINE

D

Miles

Donegal

× Ball

× Ballyshan

Grange ×

castle +

Killalla +

Dromora +

S

L. Ballysdare

Sligo

Manar

Hamilton

Crevela

Drumahare

55

Go to page 56 ▷

Go to page 59 ▽

Leraine
Ballycastle
Ballymoney
Clogh
Ballymena
Drumsough Junc.
Dunadry
Antrim
Ballypatlady
Ballynure
Carrickfergus
Carrickf. Junc.
Whiteabbey
Greencastle
Castleburgh
Bleberstane
Belfast
Dunmurry
Holywood
Newtown Ards
Lisburn
Comber
Lurgan
Tanderagee and Gulford
Killyleagh
Downpatrick
Banbridge
Poyntzpass

CAN
BUTARRAN
Kilmory
Southend
Gir
129 Miles to Glasgow
Port Patrick
New Engla
Cair
W
Donaghadee

Go to page 52

PASS OF SALRUC

ERRIVE

Go to page 55

Go to page 60

Go to page 63

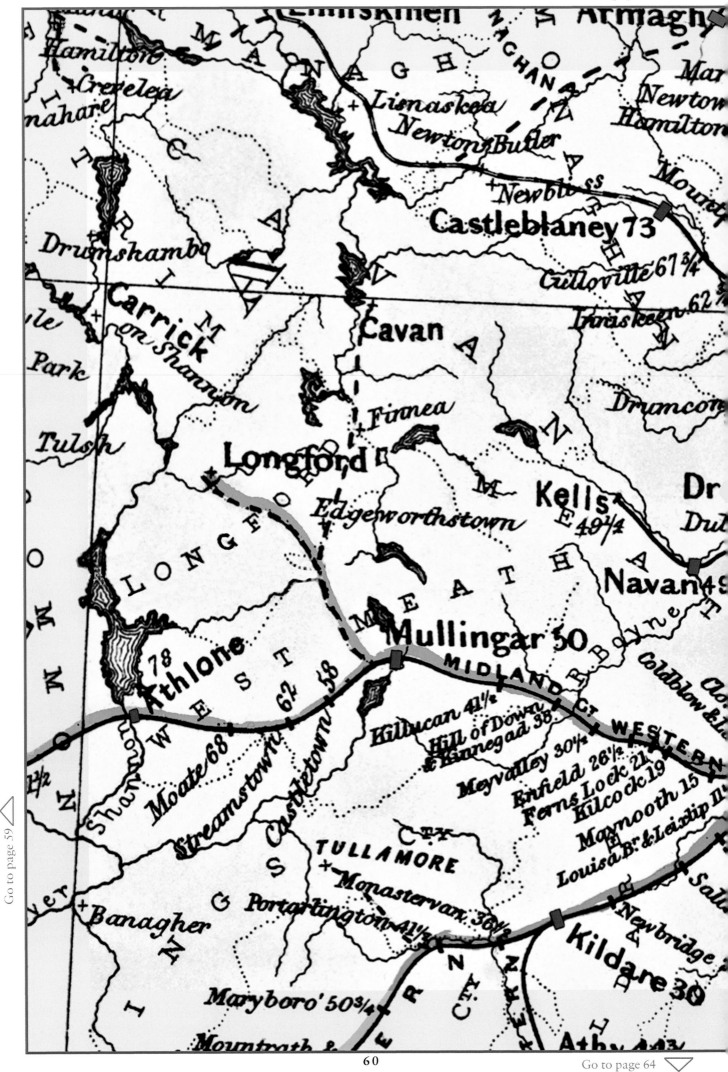

Go to page 56

Hamilton
+Crevelea
nahare+
Drumshambo
Carrick
on Shannon
Park
Tulsh
Longford
Edgeworthstown
LONG
78
Athlone
WEST
Moate 68
62
58
Streamstown
Castletown
TULLAMORE
+Monastervan 36½
+Banagher
Portarlington 41½
Maryboro' 50¾
Mountrath &

ENNISKILLEN
MANAGH
Lisnaskea
Newton Butler
+Newbliss
Castleblaney 73
Culloville 67¾
Enniskeen 62½
Cavan
A N
Firnea
Drancon
Kells
49¼
Navan 49
Mullingar 50
MIDLAND GT WESTERN
Killucan 41½
Hill of Down
& Kinnegad 38
Meyvalley 30¾
Enfield 26½
Ferns Lock 21
Kilcock 19
Maynooth 15
Louisa Br. & Leixlip 11½
Newbridge
Kildare 30
Armagh
Mar
Newtow
Hamilton
Mount
Dr
Dul
Coldblow &
Sal
Athy

Go to page 59

Go to page 64

Go to page 57

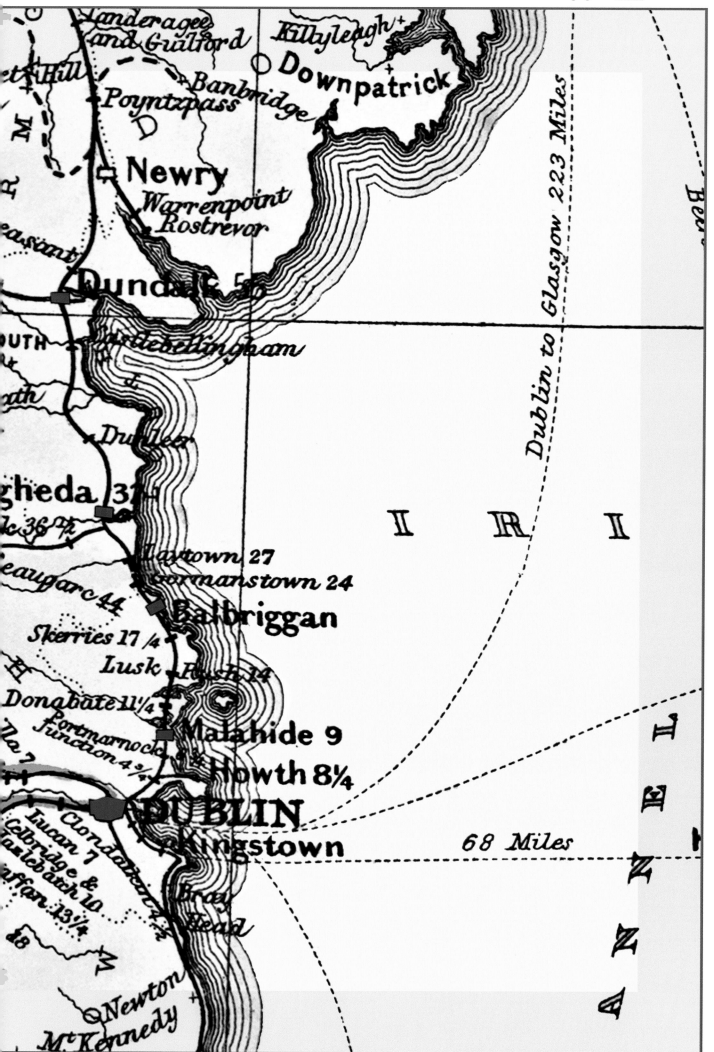

Tanderagee
and Gulford

Killyleagh +

Downpatrick +

Banbridge

Poyntzpass

D

Newry

Warrenpoint
Rostrevor

Dundalk 5½

OUTH

Castlebellingham

Dunleer

gheda 31

ck 36 ¾

Beaugarc 44

Raytown 27

Gormanstown 24

Balbriggan

Skerries 17 ¼

Lusk Rush 14

Donabate 11¼

Portmarnock
Junction 4¾

Malahide 9

Howth 8¾

na 7

DUBLIN

Clondalkin

Lucan 7

Kingstown

Celbridge &
Charlebanch 10

Naffan 13¼

Bray

Head

I R I

Dublin to Glasgow 223 Miles

E L

N

68 Miles

Newton

McKennedy

A

Z

Bea

Go to page 65

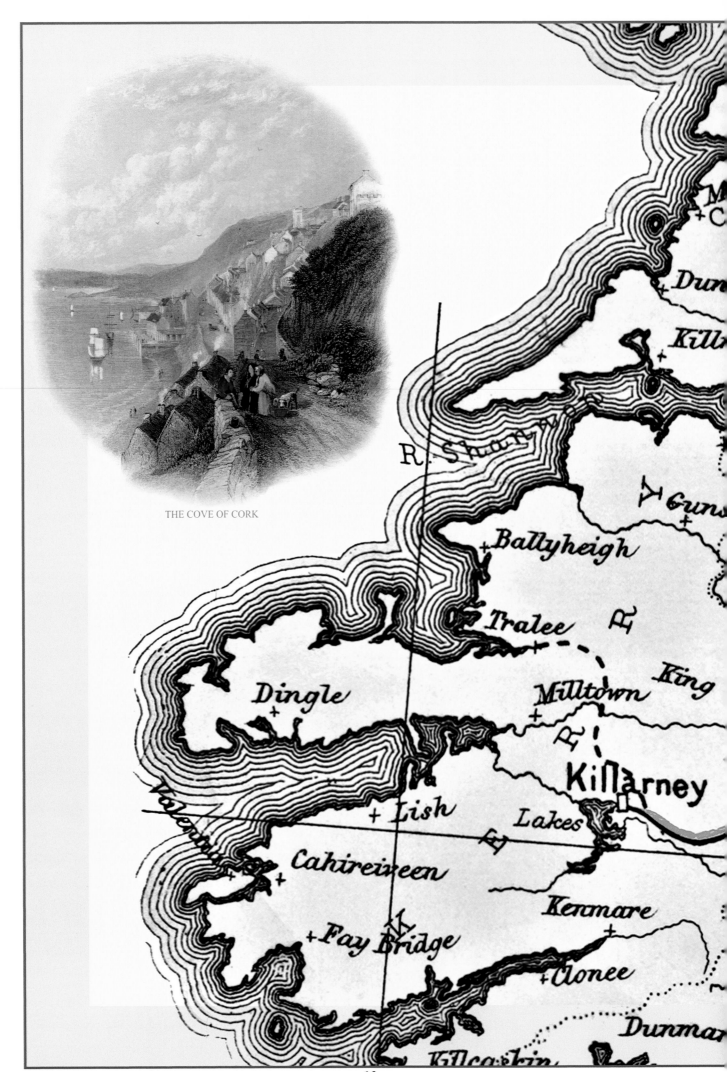

THE COVE OF CORK

R. Shan[non]

Guns[...]

Ballyheigh

Tralee

King

Milltown

Dingle

Killarney

Lish

Lakes

Cahireiveen

Kenmare

Fay Bridge

Clonee

Dunmar[...]

Killaskin

62

Go to page 66

Go to page 67 ▽

Go to page 64 ▷

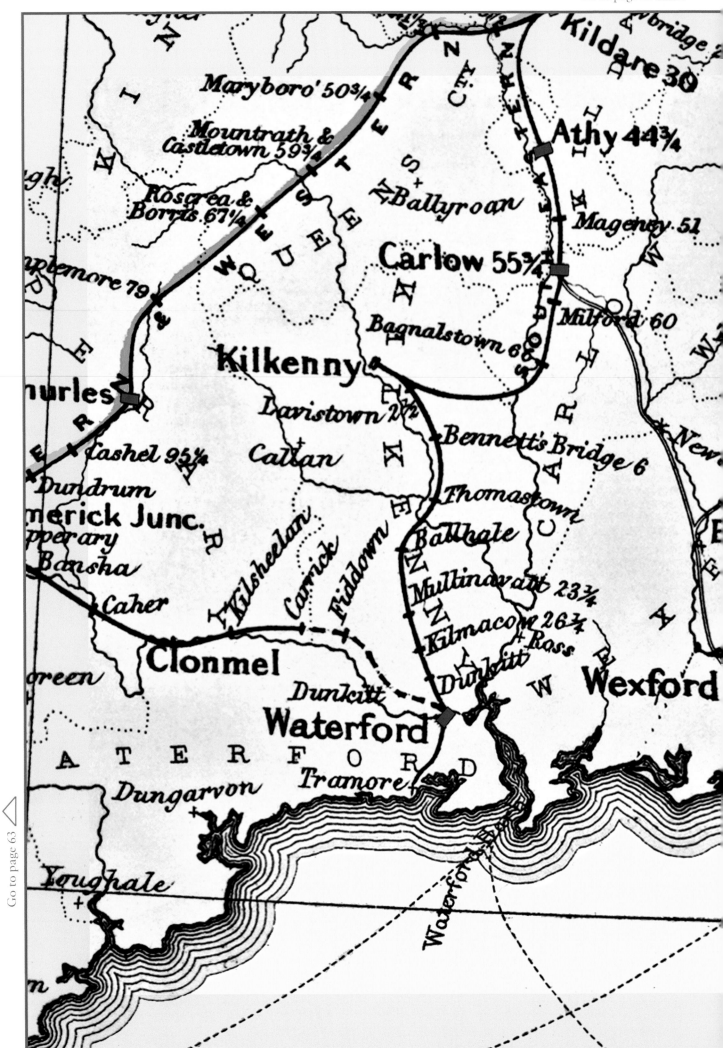

Go to page 63 ◁

Newton
Mc Kennedy
Rathdangan
Wicklow
Rathdrum
Arklow
rehely
Gorey
Barry
niscorthy
ord Harb.

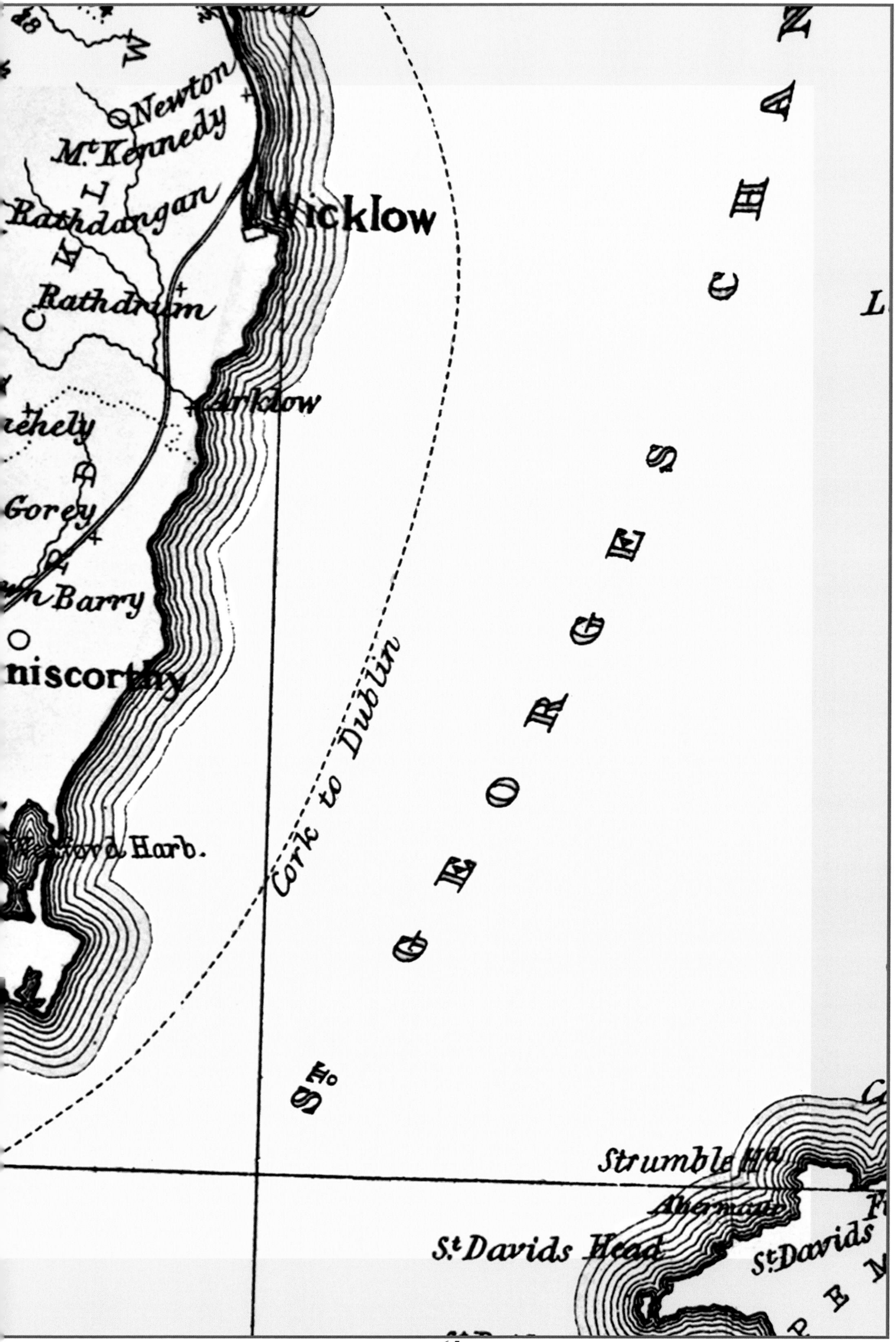

Cork to Dublin

G E O R G E S
C H A N N E L

L

S
Fo

Strumble Hd
Abermaur
St Davids Head   St Davids

BLACK ROCK CASTLE

BANTRY BAY

BLARNEY CASTLE

Go to page 63

PASSAGE

THE QUAY AT WATERFORD

LISMORE CASTLE

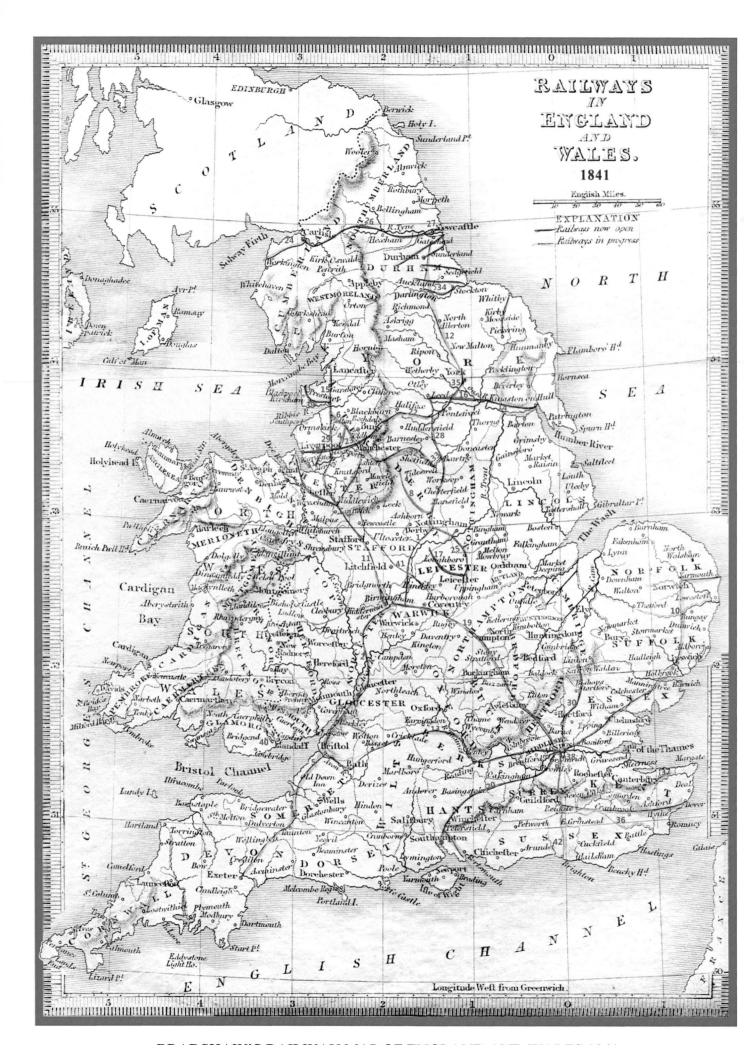

BRADSHAW'S RAILWAY MAP OF ENGLAND AND WALES 1841

Two

BRADSHAW'S ENVIRONS MAPS

An earlier George Bradshaw map of England and Wales from his "Railway Companion" published in February 1841 is featured on the adjacent page; the London Environs map from George Bradshaw's first Railway Map of Great Britain, published in 1839 is featured below. This inclusion enables at a glance a rapid development of railways in just over 10 years to when his 1852 Railway Map of Great Britain and Ireland was published. The fascinating Environs maps from London, Birmingham, Manchester, Liverpool, Leeds, Edinburgh and Glasgow, taken from that railway map follow, now enhanced in full colour. They show surrounding villages, many swallowed up as towns grew outwards forming the conurbations of today, and the railways snaking their way inwards to their magnificent stations, delivering visitors to the very heart of suburbia.

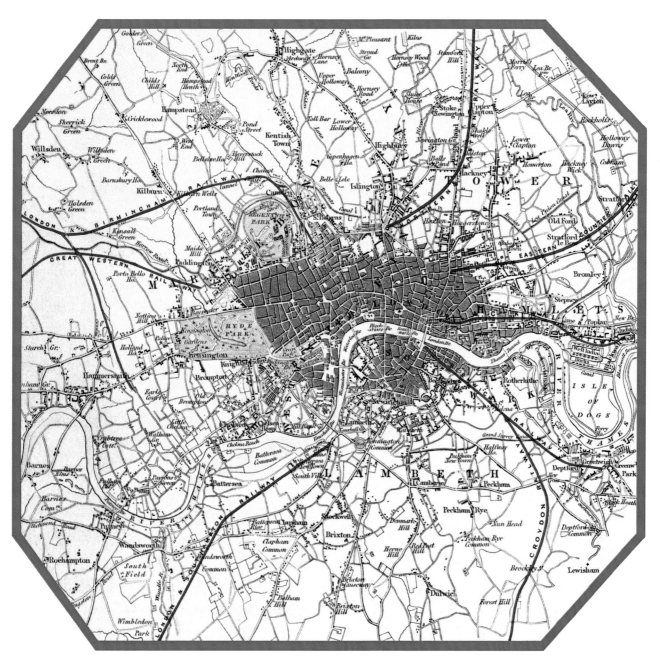

BRADSHAW'S ENVIRON'S PLAN OF LONDON RAILWAYS - 1839

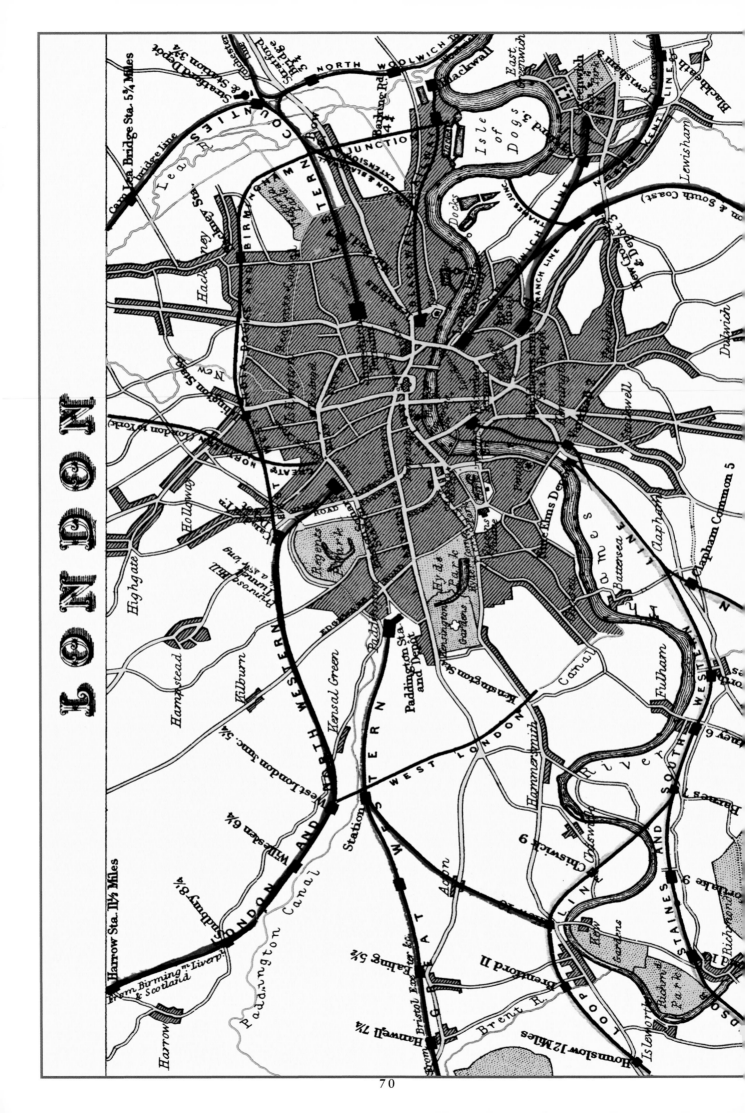

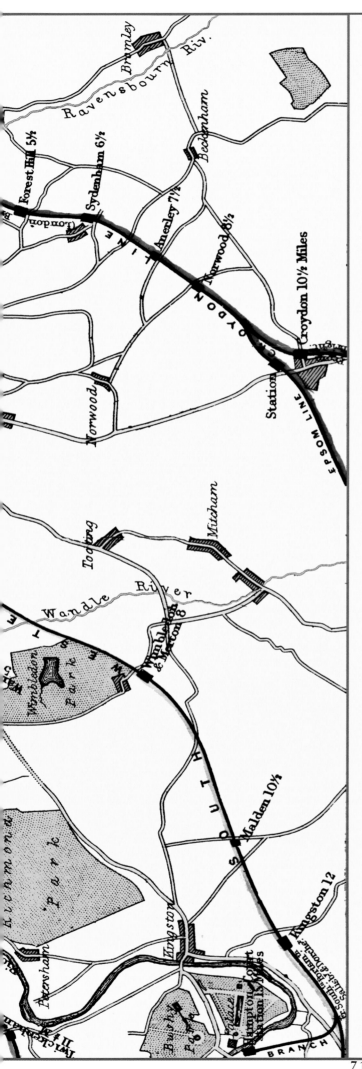

Forest Hill 5½

Sydenham 6½

Anerley 7½

Norwood 8½

Croydon 10½ Miles

Bromley

Ravensbourn Riv.

Beckenham

(London)

CROYDON LINE

EPSOM LINE

Station

Norwood

Norwood

Mitcham

Tooting

Wandle River

Wimbledon & Merton 8

Wimbledon Park

Richmond Park

Bushey Park

Malden 10½

Kingston 12

Kingston

Petersham

Twickenham

BRANCH

BUCKINGHAM PALACE

NELSON'S COLUMN

TOWER

ST PAUL'S CATHEDRAL

WESTMINSTER ABBEY

ENTRANCE TO THE LONDON AND NORTH WESTERN STATION - EUSTON SQUARE C1850

LONDON AND BIRMINGHAM RAILWAY

INTERIOR OF THE NEW GREAT CIRCULAR ENGINE HOUSE AT THE CAMDEN-TOWN DEPOT OF THE NORTH WESTERN RAILWAY, 1847

VIEW OF THE MANUFACTURING TOWN OF BIRMINGHAM, 1850

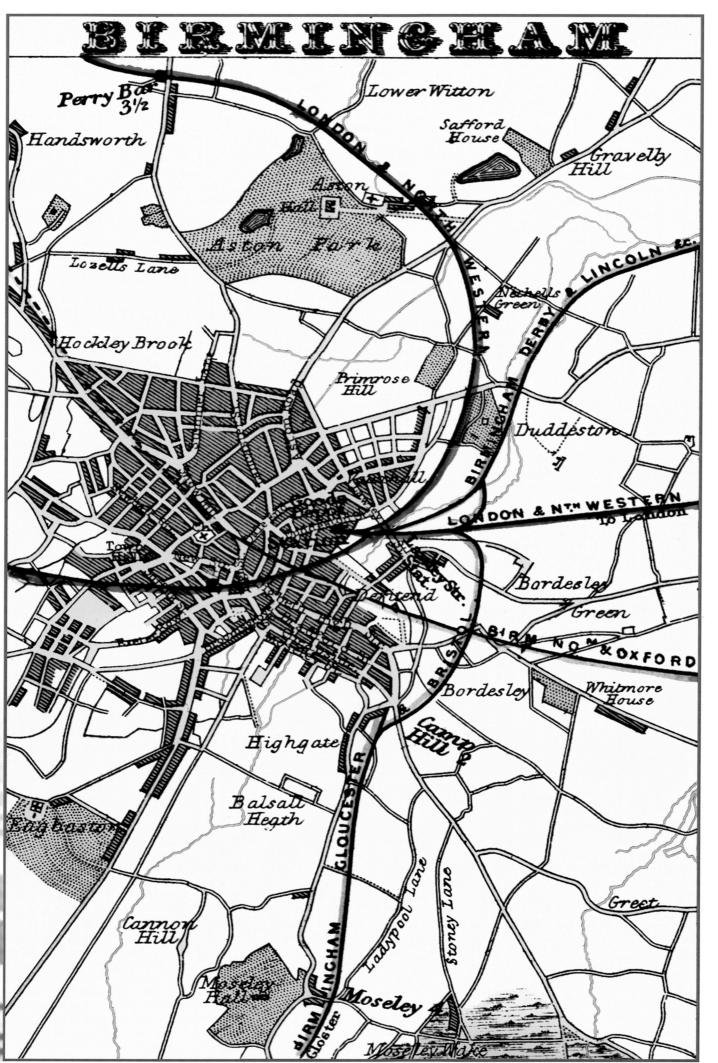

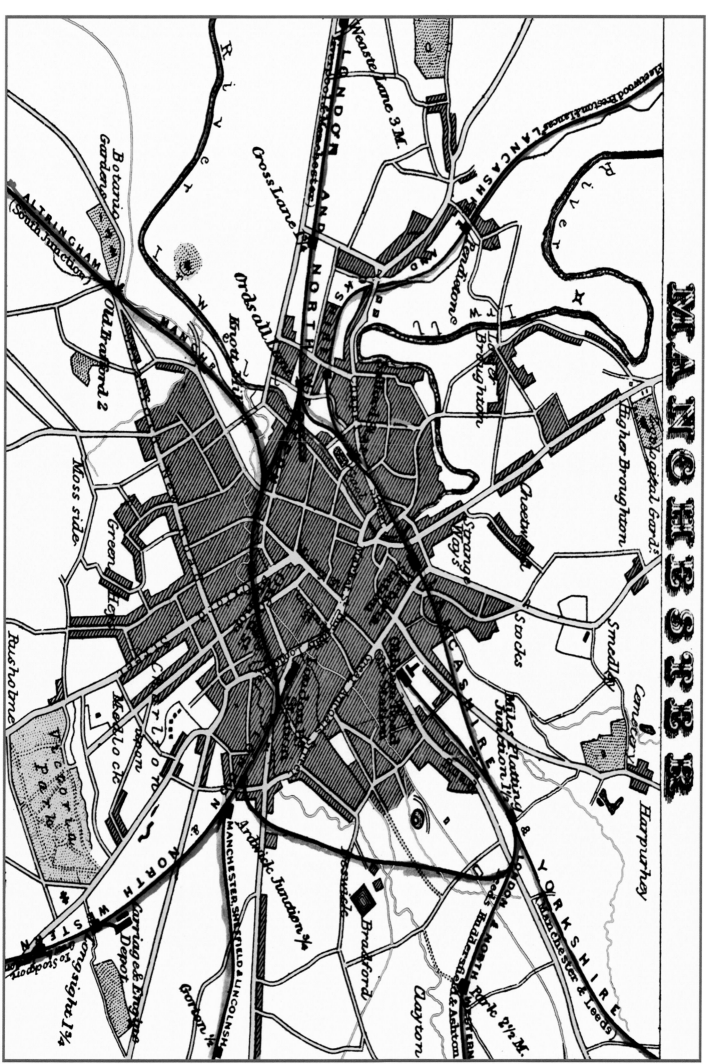

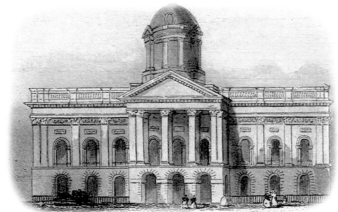

TOWN HALL

ST LUKE'S

ROYAL BANK

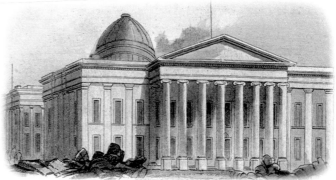

CUSTOM HOUSE

EXCHANGE

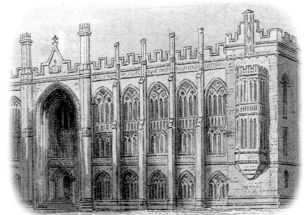

COLLEGE

ST NICHOLAS

ST GEORGE'S HALL

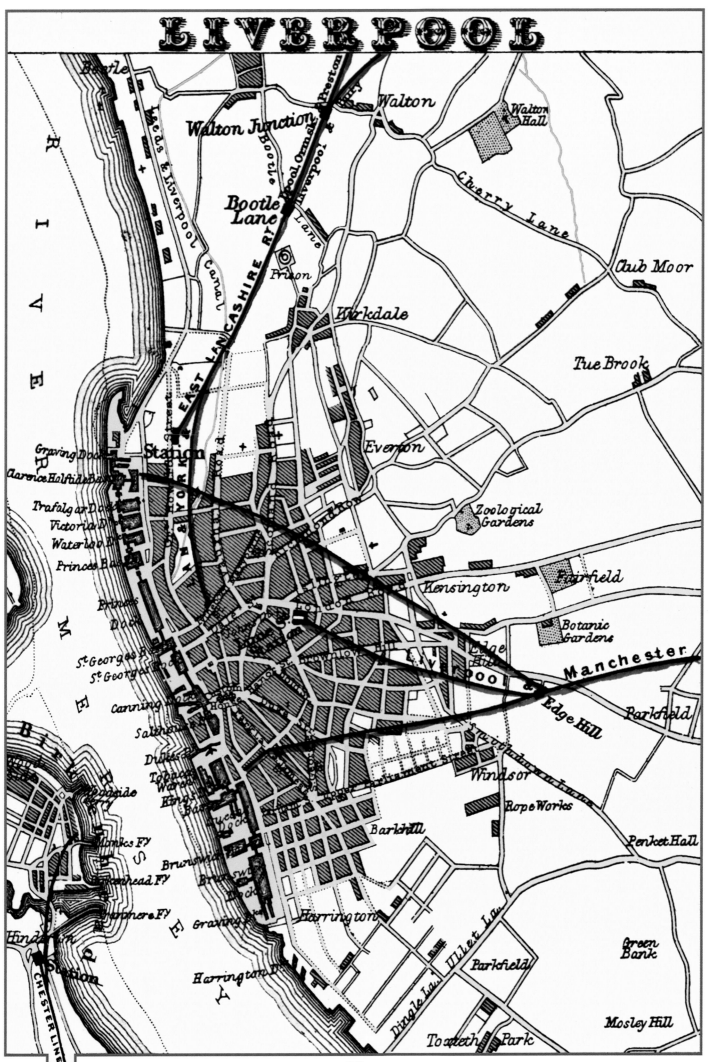

THE AIRE AND CALDER AT LEEDS, 1829

80

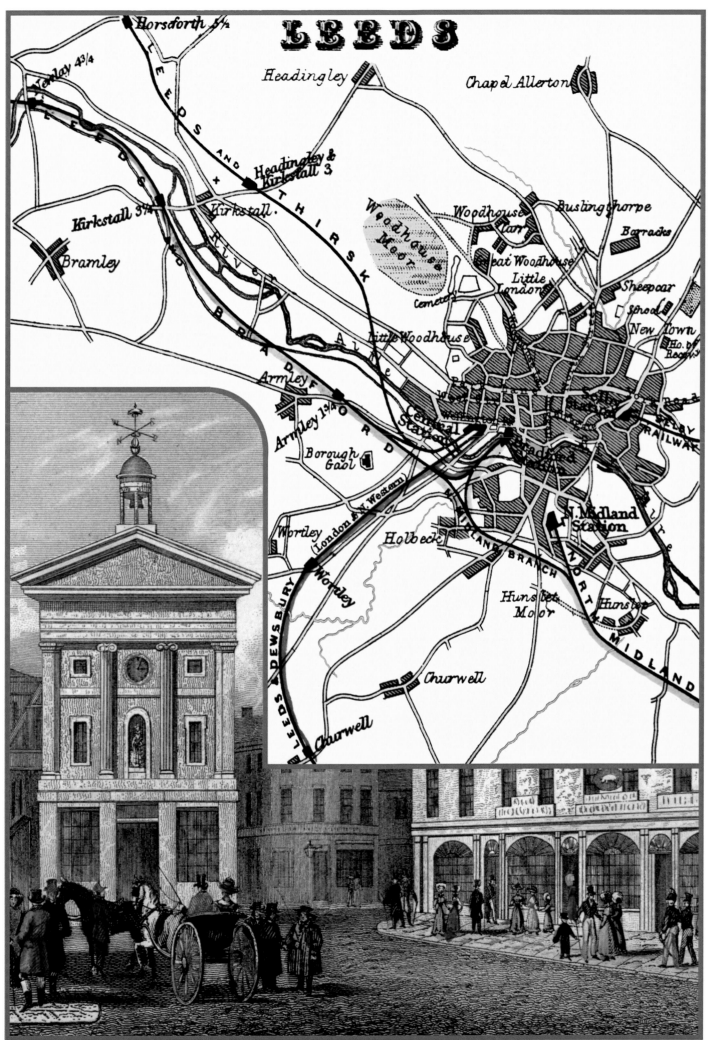

THE CORN EXCHANGE - LEEDS, 1829

THE ENTRANCE TO LOCH GOIL

LOCH GOIL HEAD

THE KYLES OF BUTE

LOCH FAD. BUTE - ARRAN IN THE DISTANCE

THE PATH BY THE LAKE - LOCH KATRINE

IN THE PASS OF THE TROSACHS

BEN LOMOND FROM TARBET

LOCH TUMMEL - THE QUEEN'S VIEW

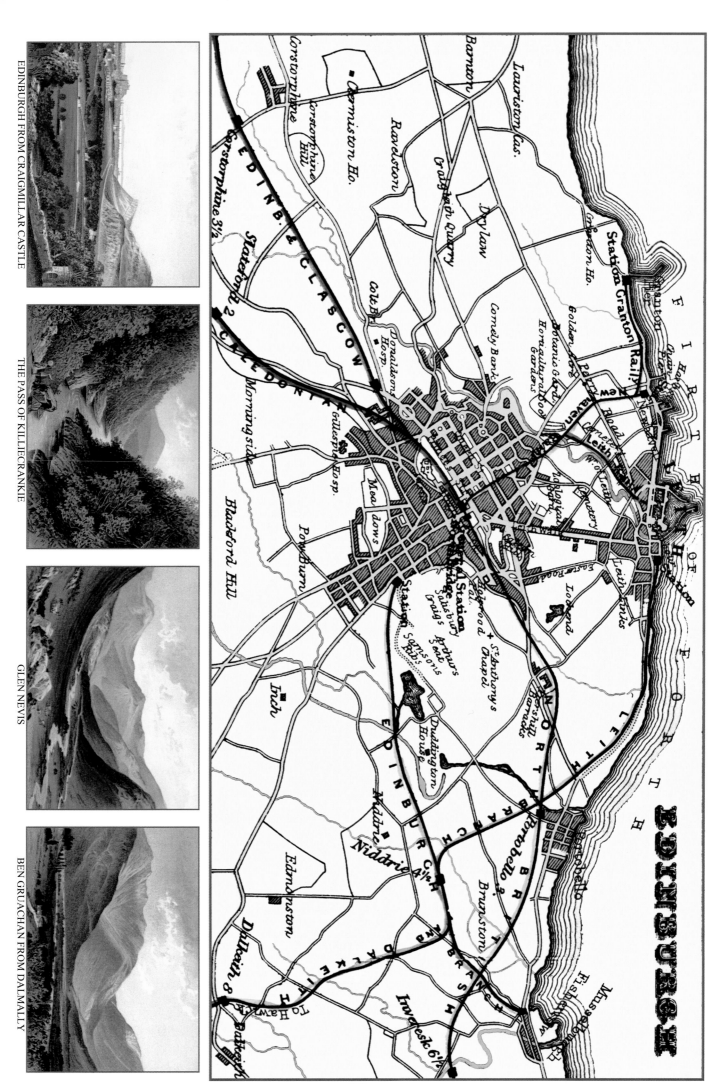

EDINBURGH FROM CRAIGMILLAR CASTLE

THE PASS OF KILLIECRANKIE

GLEN NEVIS

BEN GRUACHAN FROM DALMALLY

LOCH VENNACHER

84

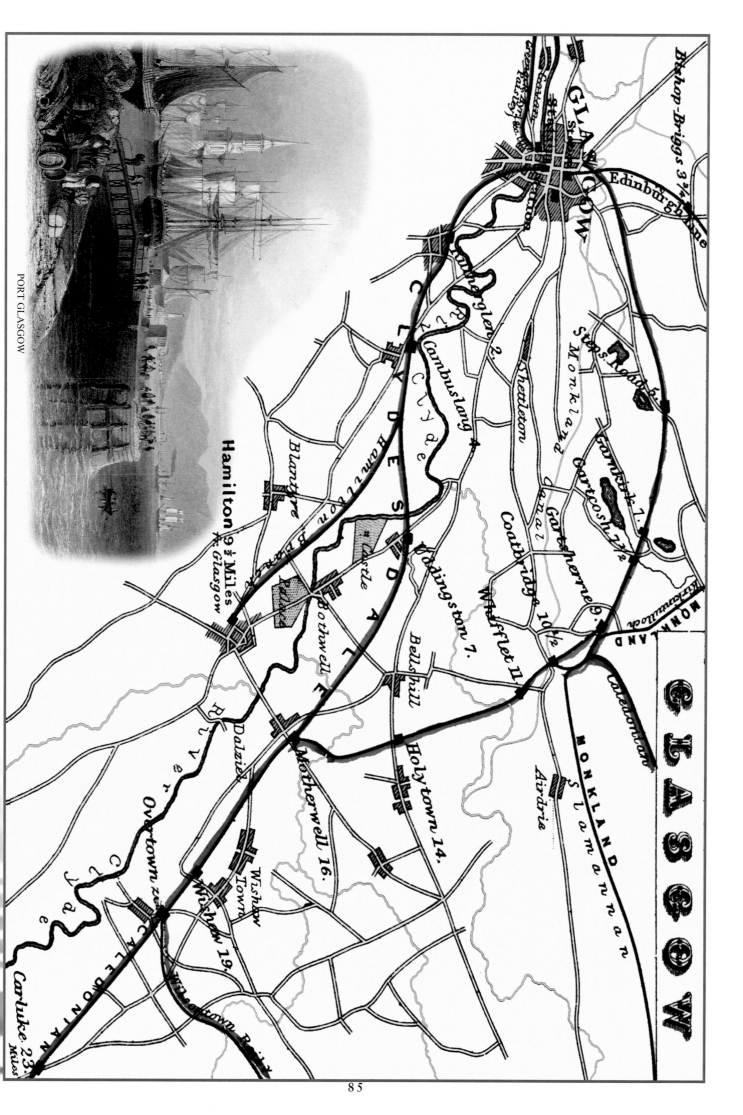

PORT GLASGOW

Bishop-Briggs 3¾

GLASGOW

St.

Edinburgh ...

Greenock 24. &c.
Cumbernauld ...

Springburn

Possil

Stobs Road

Shettleton

Monkland

Gartshoch 7.

Cambuslang 4.

Cumbernauld

MONKLAND

Monkland Canal

Gartsherrie 9.

Coatbridge 10½

Woofflet 11.

Gutcosh 7½

CALEDONIAN

Uddingston 7.

Bellshill

Caledonian

MONKLANNAN

Airdrie

CLYDE

Cambuslang

Castle

Bothwell

Dalzell

Holytown 14.

Wishaw 19.

Motherwell 16.

Wishaw Town

Hamilton 9¾ Miles
to Glasgow

Blantyre

River

Overtown ...

Clyde

CALEDONIAN

Carluke 23.
Miles

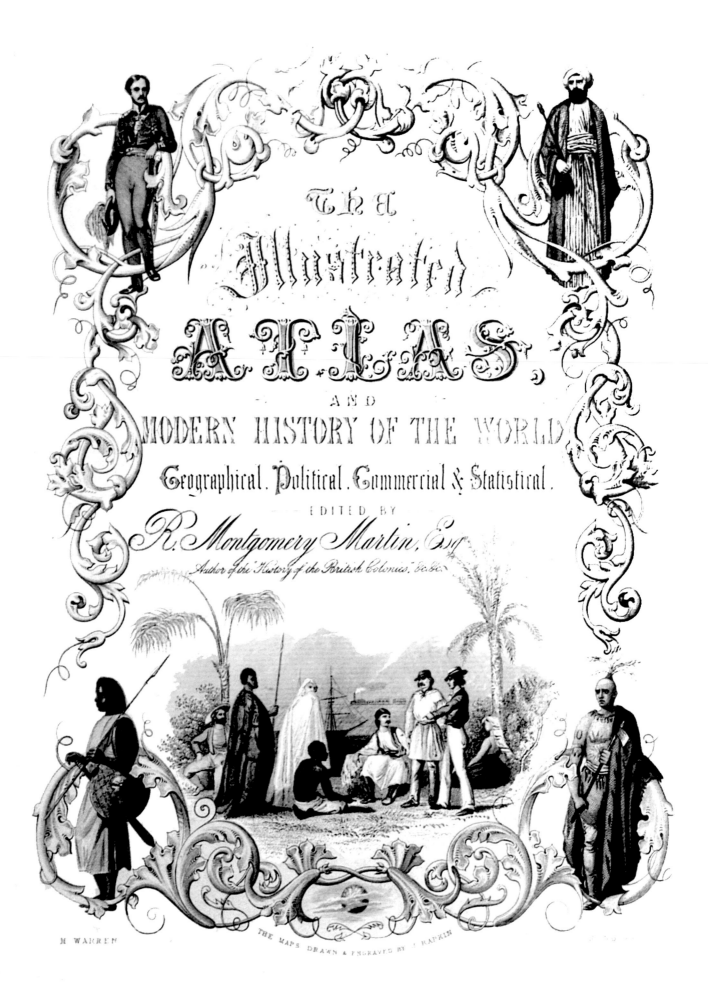

The Illustrated ATLAS,

AND
MODERN HISTORY OF THE WORLD
Geographical. Political. Commercial & Statistical.

EDITED BY

R. Montgomery Martin, Esq.

Author of the "History of the British Colonies," &c. &c.

M. WARREN

THE MAPS DRAWN & ENGRAVED BY J. RAPKIN

PRINTED AND PUBLISHED BY

THE LONDON PRINTING AND PUBLISHING COMPANY.

Three

TALLIS TOWN PLANS

The early life of John Tallis is somewhat lost to the ages - he was born in 1813 to a modest family in London, his father a shoemaker, but little else is known about his early life, schooling and career. However, an inauspicious start proved no obstacle to success, and what should always be known about Tallis is that he went on to adeptly forge a new type of business in producing and publishing exquisite maps of the world. Fascinated with travel - a committed writer of travelogues - Tallis was a man who really did map an age, innovating in achieving this on a global scale for the first time, thereby building his standing and reputation as one of the foremost cartographers and publishers of the Victorian era before his death in 1899. He ran his firm, based in London and New York, with four of his sons and traded under several names, but it was always essentially known as John Tallis & Company, active between 1838 and 1851, with other outlets publishing work thereafter.

Tallis' crowning glory was his Illustrated Atlas of the World, published between 1849 and 1853 in limited edition runs. It marked a hugely ambitious attempt to map the globe, including the recently discovered - to European minds at least - country of Australia, along with far flung, exotic places like Japan and North America. The maps contained in the atlas were of the highest quality, painstakingly and finely engraved on steel and featured attractive and vivid illustrative vignette views, giving the viewer real and absorbing insights into the people, topography, flora and fauna of the world. Issued in around 70 parts, the maps were as informative as they were supremely decorative, with much of the illustrative work carried out by a team of 20 artists led by John Rapkin.

LONDON 1851

As well as the many country maps, Tallis' Illustrated Atlas of the World also contained 22 detailed town plans from around Britain, as well as a plan of New York and Boston in the USA, which pre-date the standard Ordnance Survey maps we rely on today. The plates from the atlas are now highly collectable - the town plans in particular and widely sought after. Unfortunately, original and complete versions have become extremely rare, the vast majority stripped for sale in individual lots by antique map dealers and collectors. Given this, it is remarkable that the Tallis town plans of Britain presented in this volume are all taken from an original atlas of 1851, drawn in turn from the Mapseeker archive that has been carefully compiled over the past 25 years. Digitized and fully artworked for the first time – any creasing, stains and other inevitable signs of age from the originals carefully removed using such techniques – they are exclusively presented here, recompiled together in atlas form for the first time in an age. They give a wonderful, fresh insight into the era that Tallis did so much to set down for posterity. As such, it seems only fitting that these wonderful town plans showing the intricate railway network into the centres of our principal towns, produced around the same time as George Bradshaw's Railway Map of Great Britain and Ireland, are included in this atlas dedicated to George Bradshaw himself as a cartographic tribute to a pioneering individual.

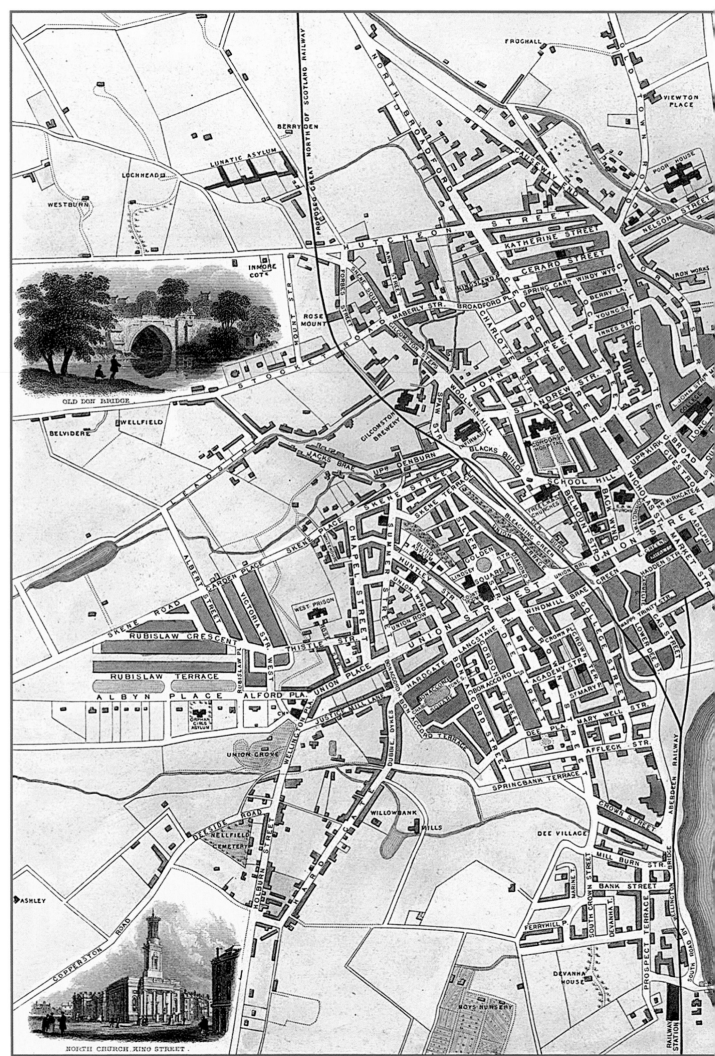

FROGHALL

VIEWTON PLACE

POOR HOUSE

NORTH OF SCOTLAND RAILWAY

BERRY DEN

LUNATIC ASYLUM

CALLSEWAY END

NELSON STREET

IRON WORKS

LOCHHEAD

WESTBURN

KATHERINE STREET

GERARD STREET

BROADFORD PL.   SPRING GARN. WINDY WYND

BROADFORD

HUTCHEON STREET

INMORE COT.

FORBES STREET

STEAL SQUARE

ANN STREET

MABERLY STR.

CHARLOTTE

BERRY LA.

YOUNG ST.

KINGSLAND PL.

INNES STR.

ROSE MOUNT

MOUNT STR.

ROAD

GILCOMSTON STEPS

JOHN   STREET

WOOLMAN HILL

ANDREW STR.

GORDON'S HOSP.

COLLEGE

OLD DON BRIDGE

BELVIDERE   WELLFIELD

STOCKET   LEADS

GILCOMSTON BREWERY

SPAW STR.

INFIRMARY ST.

BLACKS BUILD.

SCHOOL HILL

UPR KIRK C.   BROAD ST.   GUESTROW

NICHOLAS ST.

MARKET STR.

JACKS BRAE   UPR. DENBURN

FREE EAST CHURCHES

BELMONT STR.

UNION STR.

SKENE STREET   SKENE TERRACE

BLEACHING GREEN

ADELPHI

ALBERT STREET   GARDEN PLACE

SKENE PLACE

SUMMER STREET

BLIND ASYLUM

SILVER STR.

UNION TERRACE

UNION BRI.

BACK WYND

SKENE   ROAD

VICTORIA STR.

CHAPEL STREET

WEST PRISON

HUNTLEY STR.

LINDSEY

GOLDEN SQUARE

DIAMOND STR.

WINDMILL BRAE

COLLEGE STREET

MAPPS TRINITY STR.

CAS STREET

RUBISLAW CRESCENT

THISTLE STR.

UNION ROW

UNION   STREET   WEST

CROWN PL.

CROWN TER.

LOWER DEES

RUBISLAW PL.

RUBISLAW   TERRACE

UNION PLACE

BON ACCORD ST.

LANGSTANE PL.

GORDON STREET

ACADEMY ST.

MARY WELL STR.

ALBYN   PLACE   ALFORD PLA.

ORPHAN GIRLS ASYLUM

HARDGATE

BON ACCORD SQUARE

BON ACCORD STREET

ST.MARY P.

JUSTICE MILL LANE

WELLINGTON PL.

DUBBIE DYKES

BON ACCORD TERRACE

DEE PLA.

AFFLECK STR.

UNION GROVE

SPRINGBANK TERRACE

WILLOWBANK

MILLS

DEE VILLAGE

CROWN STREET

DEESIDE   ROAD

NELLFIELD CEMETERY

HOLBURN STREET

HARDGATE

MILL BURN STR.

MARINE T.

BANK STREET

WELLINGTON BRIDGE

ABERDEEN   RAILWAY

ASHLEY

COPPERSTON   ROAD

FERRYHILL P.

SOUTH CROWN STREET

DEVANHA T.

DEVANHA T.

PROSPECT TERRACE

SOUTH   ROAD

DEVANHA HOUSE

BOYS NURSERY

RAILWAY STATION

NORTH CHURCH, KING STREET.

88

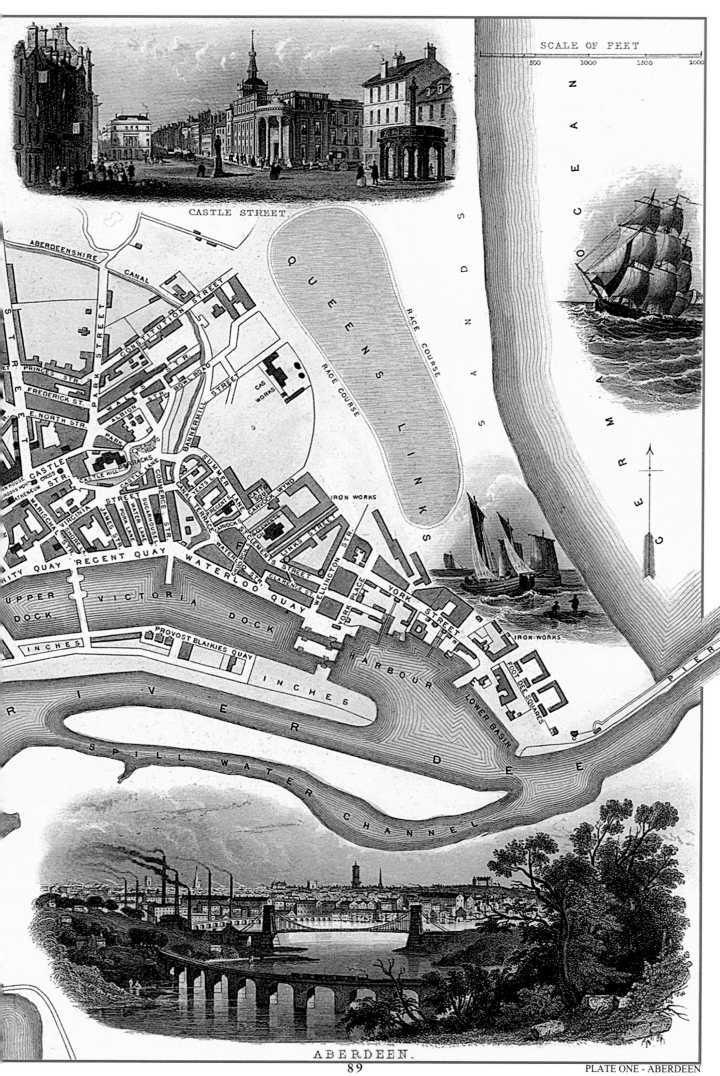

CASTLE STREET.

SCALE OF FEET

500   1000   1500   2000

O C E A N

G E R M A N

ABERDEEN.

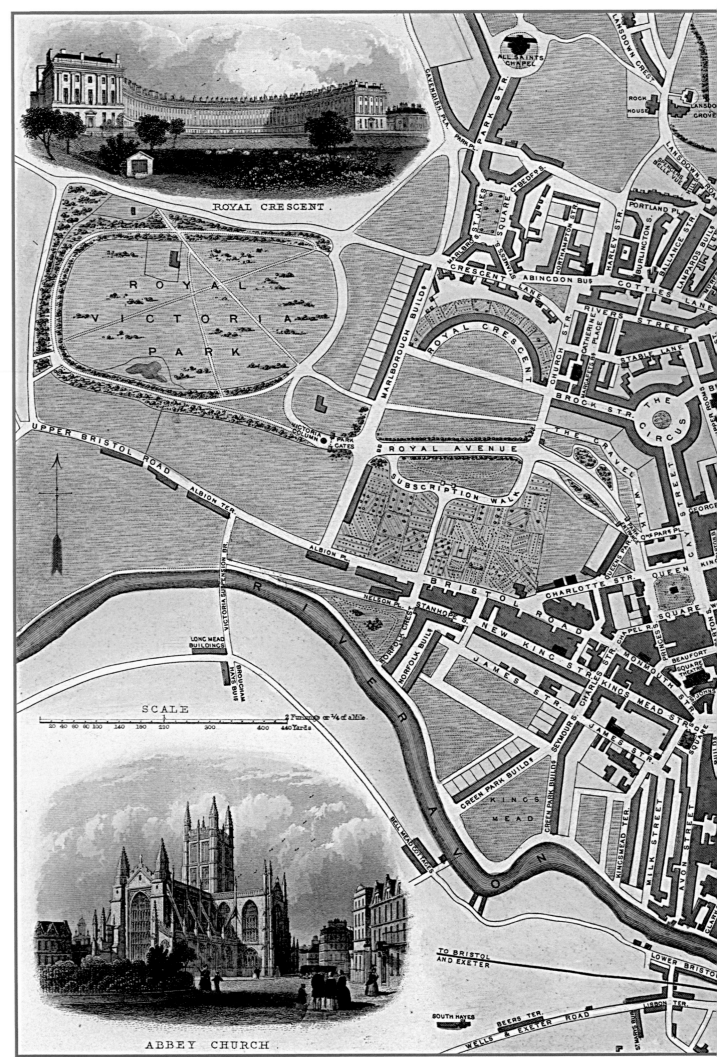

ROYAL CRESCENT.

ROYAL VICTORIA PARK

ABBEY CHURCH.

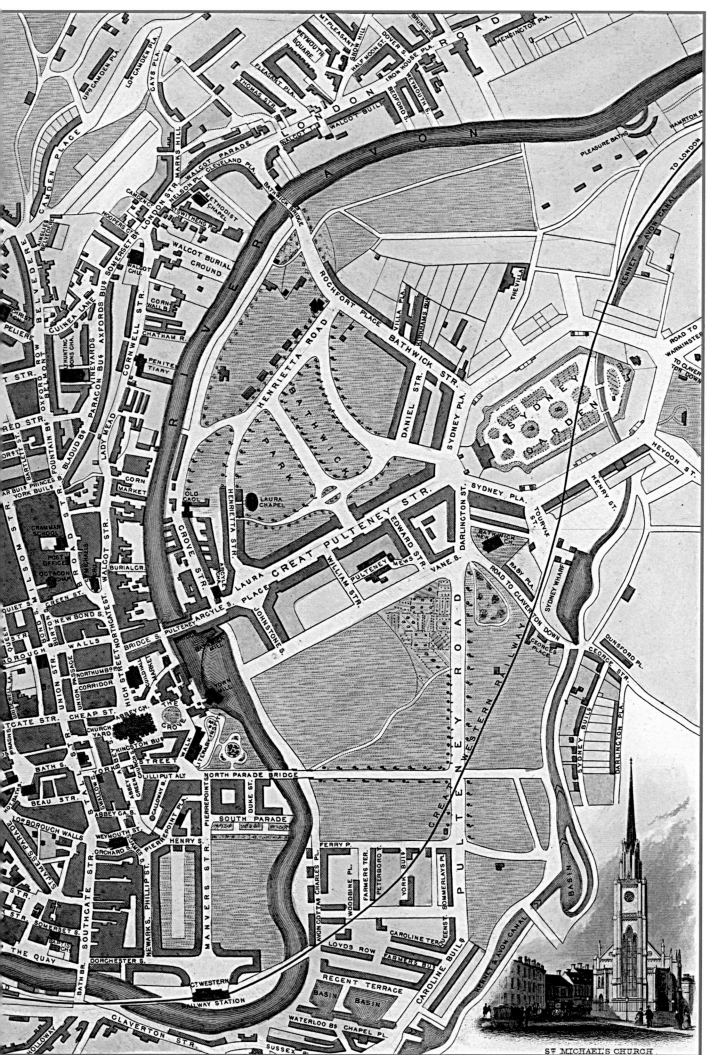

ST MICHAEL'S CHURCH

91

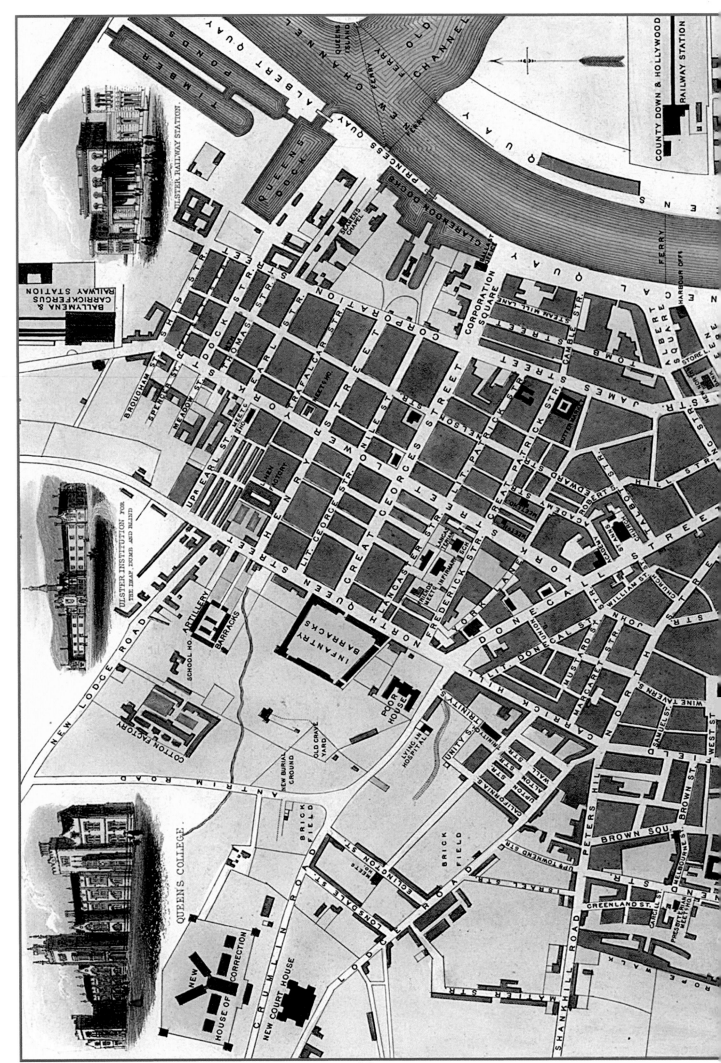

ULSTER RAILWAY STATION.

BALLYMENA & CARRICKFERGUS RAILWAY STATION

COUNTY DOWN & HOLLYWOOD RAILWAY STATION

ULSTER INSTITUTION FOR THE DEAF, DUMB AND BLIND

QUEEN'S COLLEGE.

OLD CHANNEL

QUEENS ISLAND

FERRY

FERRY

NEW CHANNEL

ALBERT QUAY

PRINCESS QUAY

QUEENS QUAY

TIMBER PONDS

QUEENS DOCKS

CLARENDON DOCKS

SEAMEN'S CHAPEL

CORPORATION SQUARE

STEAM MILL LANE

CAMBLE STR.

JAMES STREET

ALBERT SQUARE

TOMB STR.

STORE LANE

NEW LANE

HARBOUR OFFS

FERRY

CORPORATION STREET

SHIP STREET

DOCK STREET

THOMAS STREET

EARL STREET

TRAFALGAR STREET

NILE STR.

GEORGE STR.

NELSON STREET

T. PATRICK STR.

GREAT PATRICK STREET

EDWARD STR.

ACADEMY STREET

HILL STR.

TALBOT STREET

YORK STREET

BROUGHAM STR.

SPENCER STR.

MEADOW ST.

UPR EARL ST.

KENT STREET

MEETG HO.

LINEN FACTORY

HENRY STREET

LITT. GEORGE STR.

GREAT GEORGE STREET

LANCASTER STREET

FREDERICK STR.

FREDERICK ST.

METH. MEETG

INFIRMARY

LANCA TERIAN SCHOOL

GREAT PATRICK STR.

ROBERT STR.

CHURCH STR.

METHO.

DONEGALL STREET

DONEGALL STR.

WILLIAM ST.

JOHN STR.

MUSTARD STR.

MARGARET STR.

SAMUEL ST.

NORTH

ST.

NEW LODGE ROAD

SCHOOL HO.

ARTILLERY BARRACKS

INFANTRY BARRACKS

QUEEN STREET

NORTH STREET

POOR HOUSE

CARRICK HILL

WINE TAVERN STR.

WEST ST.

COTTON FACTORY

OLD GRAVE YARD

LYING IN HOSPITAL

TRINITY

UNITY ST.

WALL STR.

UPTON STR.

ALTON STR.

CALIFORNIA ST.

PETERS HILL

BROWN ST.

BROWN SQU.

ANTRIM ROAD

NEW BURIAL GROUND

BRICK FIELD

BRICK FIELD

SHANKHILL ROAD

CREENLAND ST.

CARCILL ST.

MELBOURNE ST.

PRESBYTERIAN MEETG HOUSE

CRUMLIN ROAD

NEW HOUSE OF CORRECTION

NEW COURT HOUSE

LONSDALE ST.

EGLINTON ST.

METHO.

SHANKILL ROAD

UPR TOWNEND STR.

SHAKEL STR.

WALK

QUAY

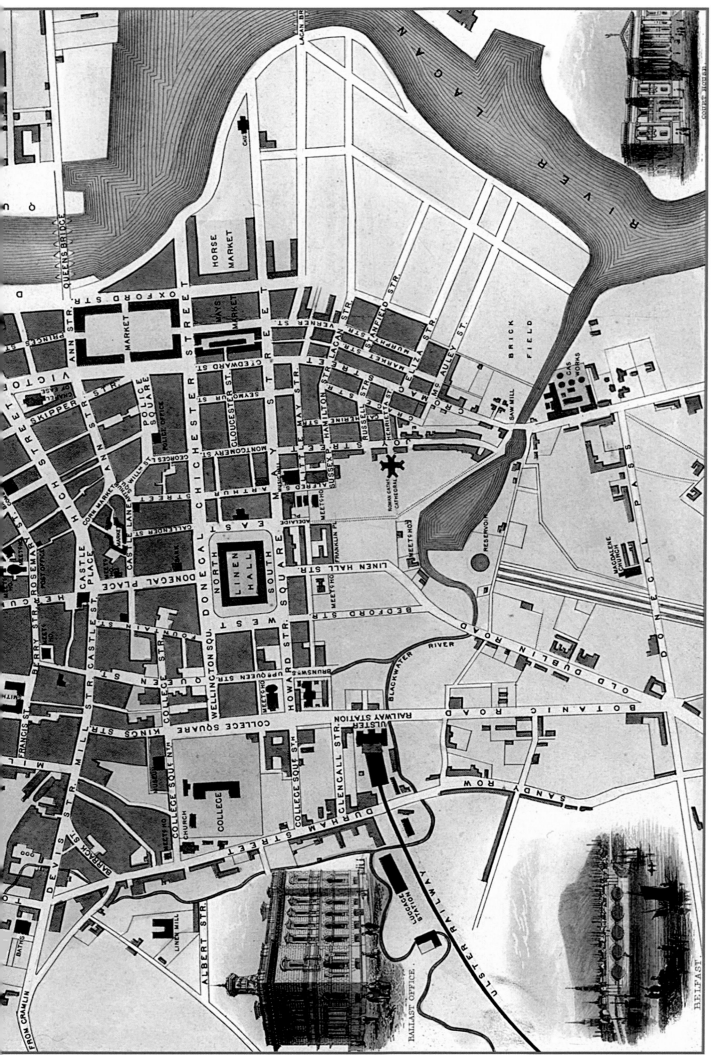

COURT HOUSE.

RIVER LAGAN

QUEENS BRIDGE

FROM CRAMLIN

HORSE MARKET

MAYS MARKET

OXFORD STR.

PRINCE'S ST.

ANN STR.

VICTOR

HALL OF EAST

SKIPPER STREET

POLICE SQUARE

POLICE OFFICE

GLOUCESTER ST.

SEYMOUR ST.

OTEDWARD ST.

CHICHESTER STREET

VERNER ST.

STANFIELD STR

MURPHY STR

ELIZA STR.

MACAULEY ST.

BRICK FIELD

GAS WORKS

SAW MILL

ST. GEORGE'S

GEORGE'S LS.

WILLS

LANE SONS

CORN MARKET

MARKET

CASTLE LANE

CASTLE PLACE

HIGH ST.

ROSEMARY

POST OFFICE

BERRY STR

MARKET

ARTHUR STREET

CALLENDER ST.

MUSIC HALL

MONTGOMERY ST.

LT LE MAY STR.

HAMILTON STR.

ALFRED S

ADELAIDE S

LACAN STR.

MARKET STR.

RUSSELL STR.

HENRIETTA ST.

CATHERINE ST.

SUSSEX P.

MEET'G HO

ROMAN CATH.
CATHEDRAL

MEET'G HO.

RESERVOIR

MAGDALENE
CHURCH

DONEGAL

OLD DUBLIN ROAD

BOTANIC ROAD

LINEN
HALL

NORTH

SOUTH

DONEGAL PLACE

FOUNTAIN

WEST

WELLINGTON SQU.

SQUARE

EAST

LINEN HALL STR.

FRANKLIN PL.

MEET'G HO.

BEDFORD STR

HOWARD STR.

BRUNSWK.

UPP QUEEN STR.

QUEEN

COLLEGE STR.

CASTLE ST.

MILL STR.

KINGS STR.

FRANCIS ST.

DEVIS ST.

BARRACK ST.

BLACKWATER RIVER

COLLEGE SQUARE

COLLEGE SQUE STH.

COLLEGE SQUE N.

COLLEGE
CHURCH

COLLEGE

DURHAM

CLENCALL STR.

DURHAM STREET

ALBERT STR.

LINEN MILL

BATHS

SANDY ROW

ULSTER
RAILWAY STATION

LUGGAGE
STATION

ULSTER RAILWAY

BALLAST OFFICE.

BELFAST.

93

FROM OLDBURY

THEATRE ROYAL

BIRMINGHAM FROM HIGHGATE

ST PHILIPS CHURCH

THE LONDON & NORTH WESTERN RAILWAY STATION

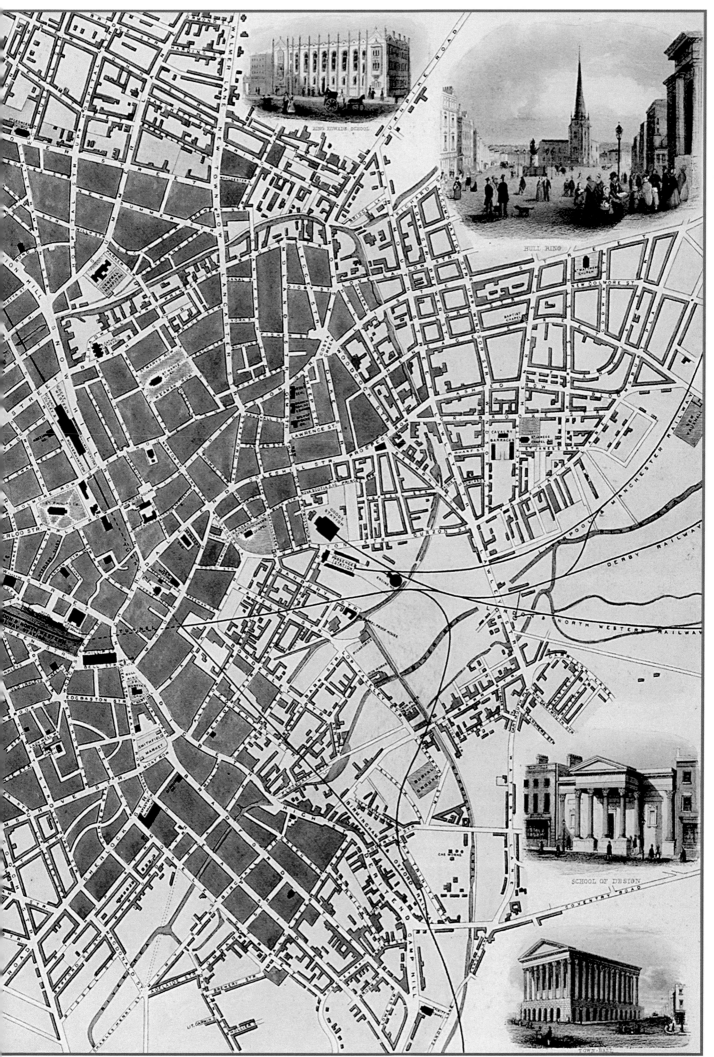

KING EDWARD'S SCHOOL

BULL RING

SCHOOL OF DESIGN

TOWN HALL

TERMINUS OF THE BRADFORD
AND HALIFAX RAILWAY

AIREDALE COLLEGE.

ST GEORGE'S HALL.

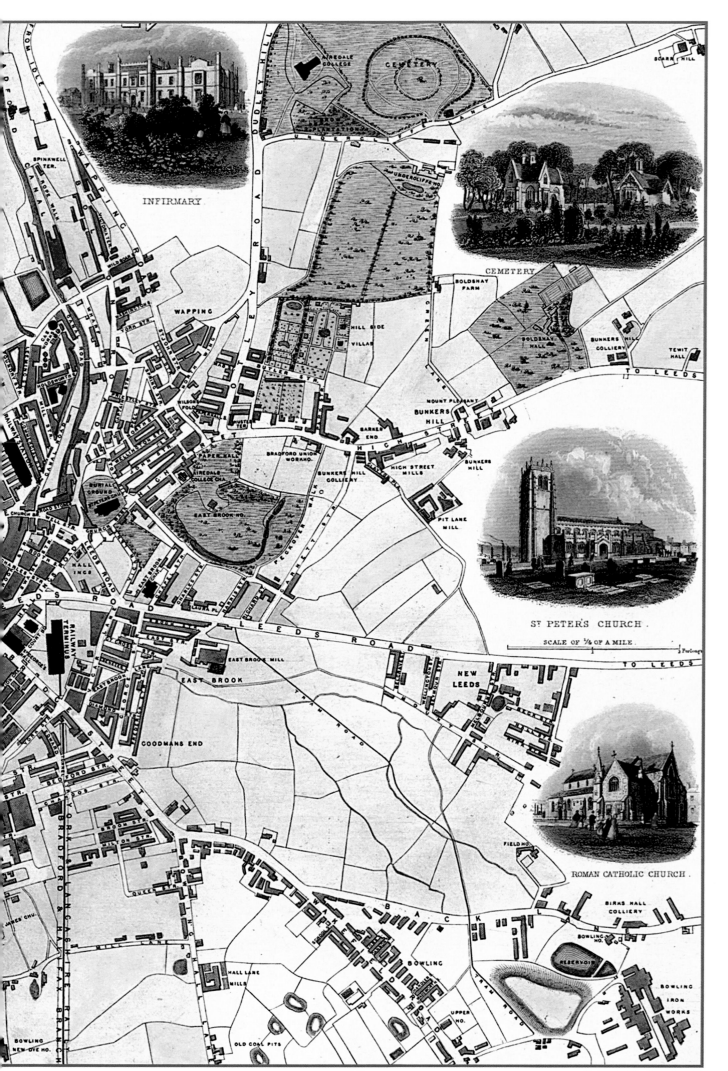

INFIRMARY

CEMETERY

ST PETER'S CHURCH.

SCALE OF ¼ OF A MILE.

ROMAN CATHOLIC CHURCH.

97   PLATE FIVE - BRADFORD

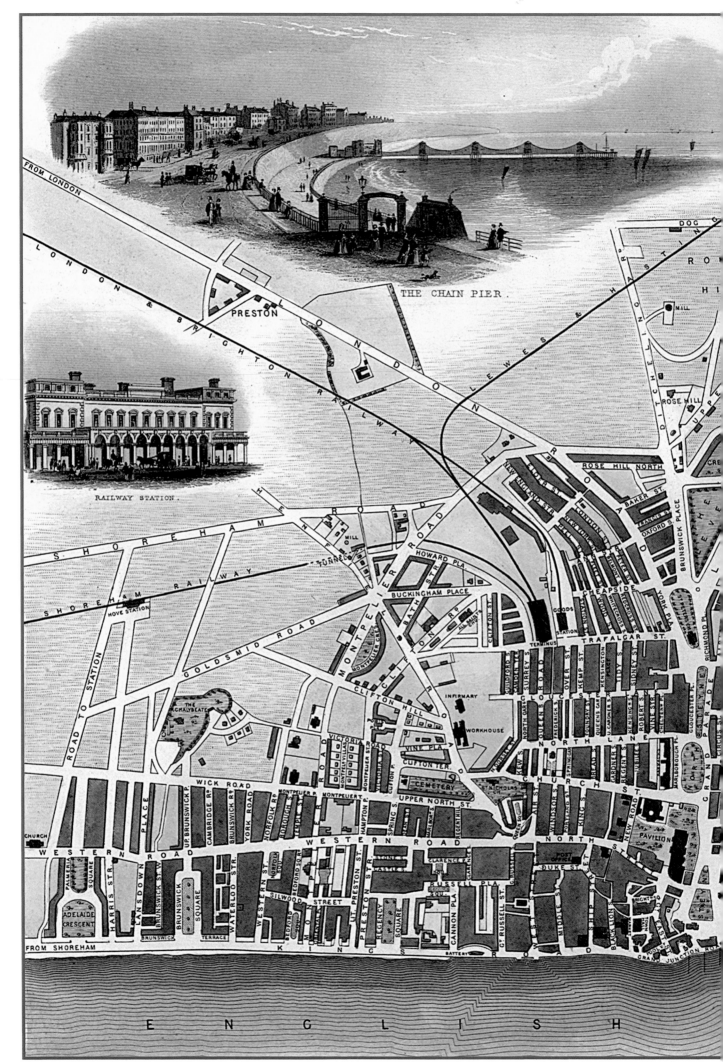

THE CHAIN PIER.

RAILWAY STATION.

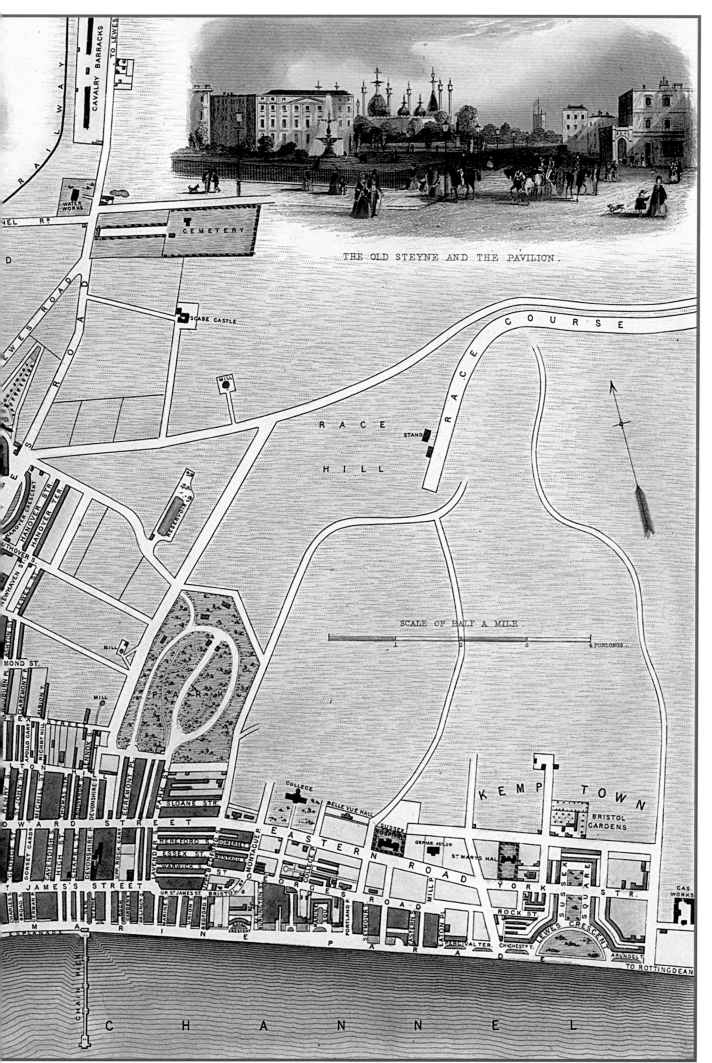

THE OLD STEYNE AND THE PAVILION.

RAILWAY

TO LEWES

CAVALRY BARRACKS

WATER WORKS

NEL Rd

LEWES ROAD

CEMETERY

SGABE CASTLE

MILL

RACE COURSE

RACE HILL

STAND

SCALE OF HALF A MILE

1   2   3   4 FURLONGS.

KEMP TOWN

PARK

BRISTOL GARDENS

COLLEGE

BELLE VUE HALL

SUSSEX HOSPITAL

ORPHAN ASYLUM

St MARYS HALL

SLOANE STR

HEREFORD St

ESSEX ST

WARWICK St

EASTERN ROAD

YORK

SUSSEX SQUARE

STR

GAS WORKS

JAMES'S STREET

UP. St JAMES St

ROCK ST.

LEWES CRESCENT

MILL

CHAIN PIER

ARUNDEL

TO ROTTINGDEAN

C H A N N E L

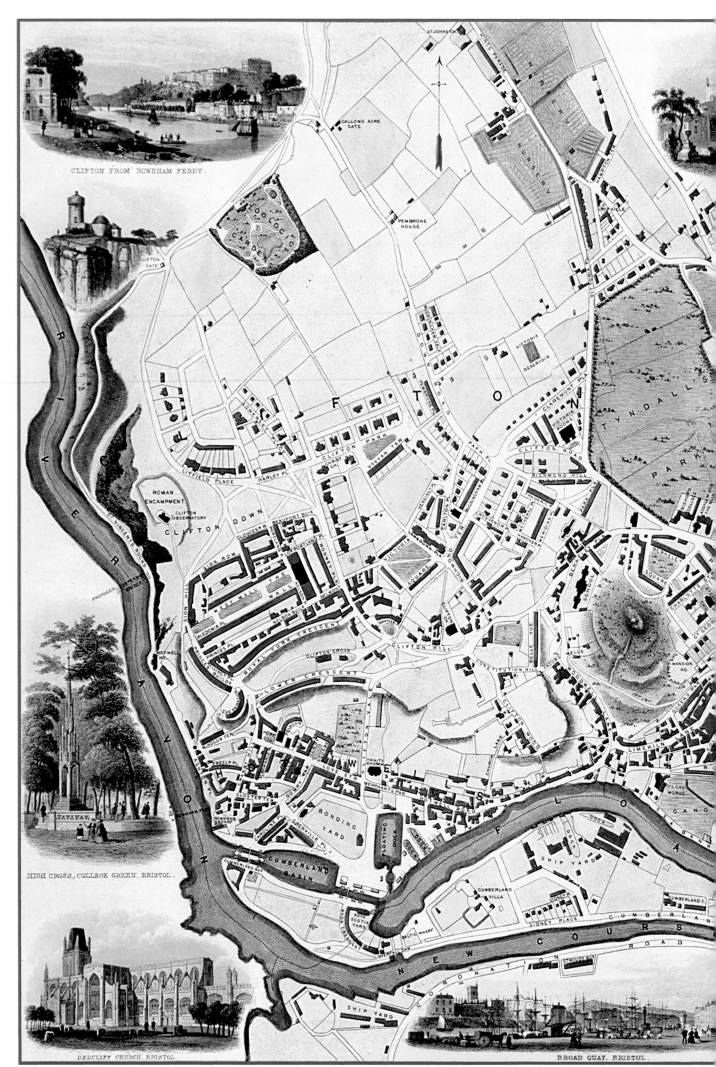

CLIFTON FROM ROWNHAM FERRY.

HIGH CROSS, COLLEGE GREEN, BRISTOL.

REDCLIFF CHURCH, BRISTOL.

BROAD QUAY, BRISTOL.

101   PLATE SEVEN - BRISTOL

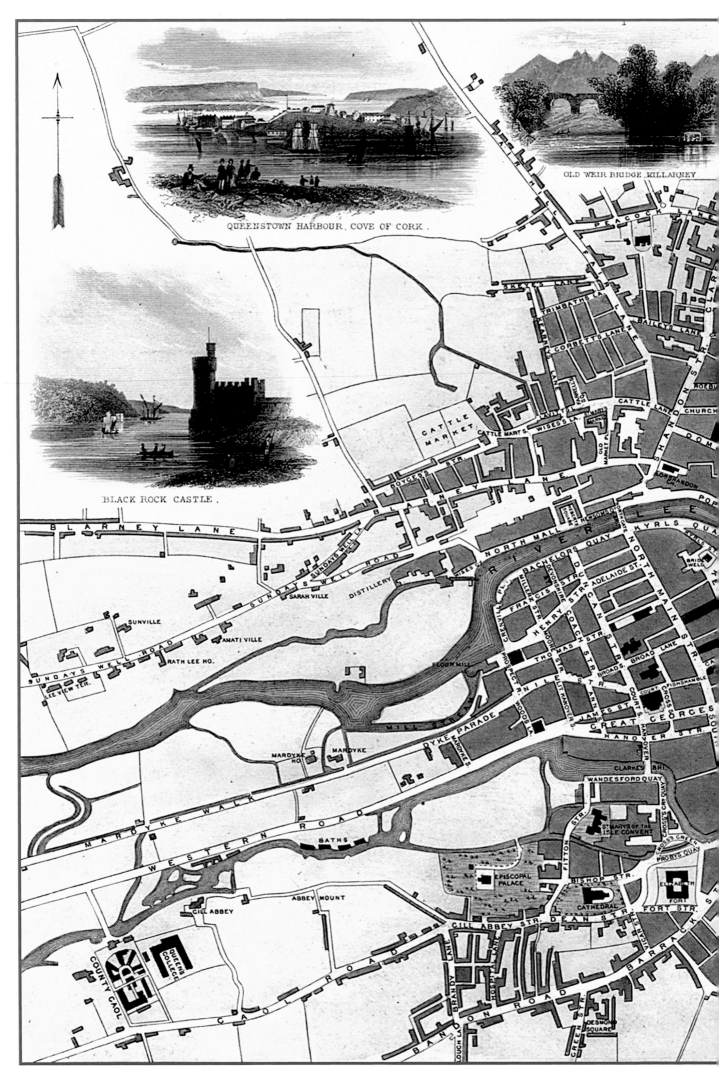

QUEENSTOWN HARBOUR, COVE OF CORK.

OLD WEIR BRIDGE, KILLARNEY.

BLACK ROCK CASTLE.

BLARNEY LANE

SUNDAYS WELL ROAD

SUNDAYS WELL LA.

SARAH VILLE

DISTILLERY

SUNVILLE

AMATI VILLE

RATH LEE HO.

SUNDAYS WELL ROAD

LEE VIEW TER.

FLOUR MILL

MILL FIELD

DYKE PARADE

MARDYKE S.

MARDYKE

MARDYKE HO.

MARDYKE WALK

WESTERN ROAD

BATHS

ABBEY MOUNT

GILL ABBEY

COUNTY GAOL

QUEENS COLLEGE

CAOL ROAD

CATTLE MARKET

CATTLE MART S.

WISE'S LA.

OLD MARKET PL.

BLARNEY LANE

ROYCES S. STR.

NORTH MALL

RIVER LEE

NORTH MAIN STR.

BACHELORS QUAY

KYRLS QUAY

WANDESFORD QUAY

CROSS GREEN

CROSS'S CH. QUAY

PROBYS QUAY

ST MARYS OF THE ISLE CONVENT

FITTON STR.

EPISCOPAL PALACE

BISHOP STR.

CATHEDRAL

FORT STR.

ELIZABETH FORT

GILL ABBEY STR.

DEAN STR.

DESMOND SQUARE

GREEN STR.

HOSPITAL LANE

BRANDY LANE

LOUGH LANE

BANDON ROAD

BARRACK STR.

GREAT GEORGES STR.

HANOVER STR.

CROSS STR.

FISHSHAMBLE

BROAD LANE

BROAD S.

COURT S.

JAMES S.

HENRY STR.

ADELAIDE ST.

COACH STR.

THOMAS STR.

DUNCAN STR.

MOORE STR.

DESMONDSHIRE STR.

FRANCIS STR.

GRENVILLE PL.

PROSPECT R.

WOODS L.

WEST HANOVER

MILLER'S STR.

CLARKES BRI.

PEACOCK LANE

SKETTS LANE

TRIMBATHS LA.

KEARNY LANE

CORBETTS LANE

CATTLE LANE

CHURCH

BAILEYS LANE

SHANDON STR.

FARRELL SQ.

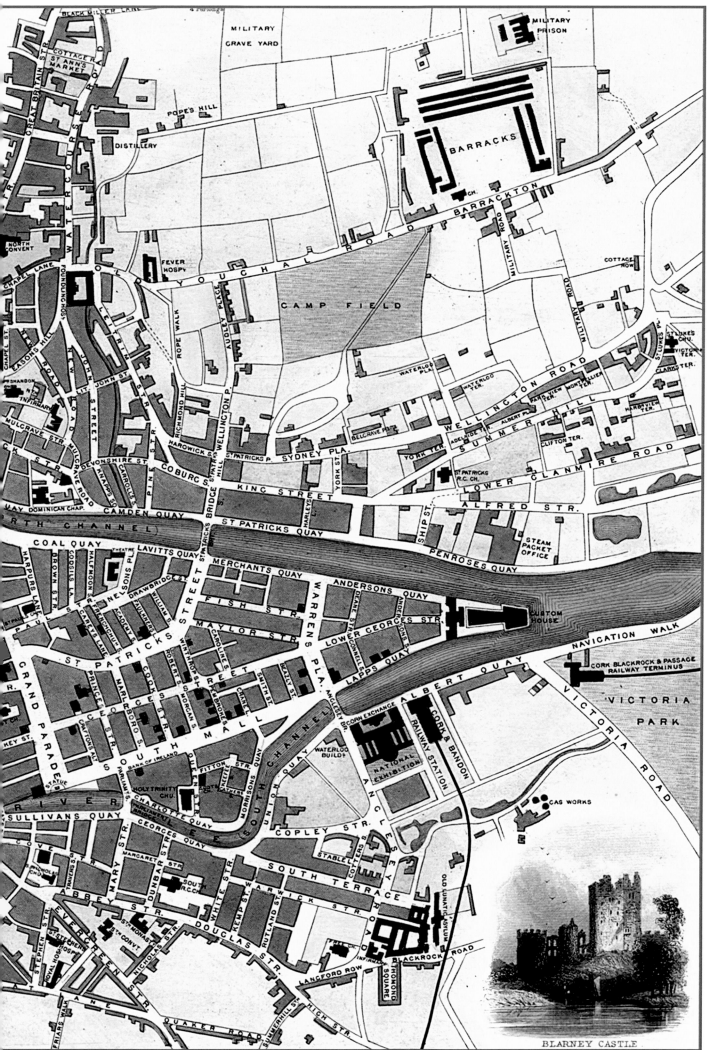

BLARNEY CASTLE

CUSTOM HOUSE.

ST. PATRICKS.

KINGS BRIDGE.

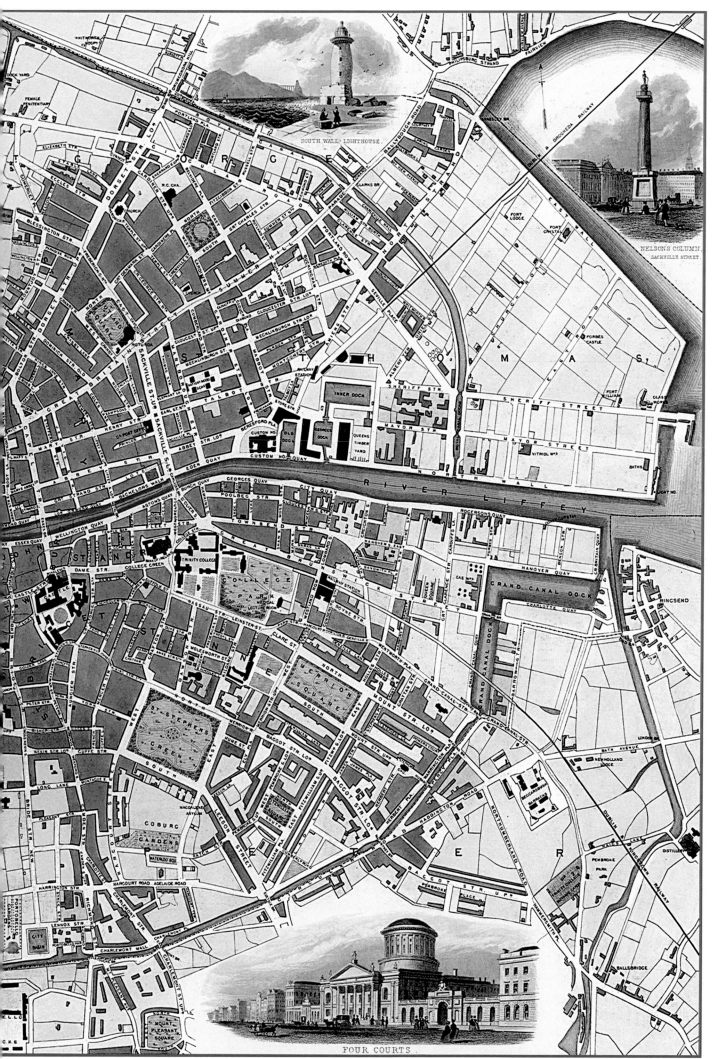

SOUTH WALL LIGHTHOUSE.

NELSON'S COLUMN.
SACKVILLE STREET.

FOUR COURTS.

PLATE NINE - DUBLIN

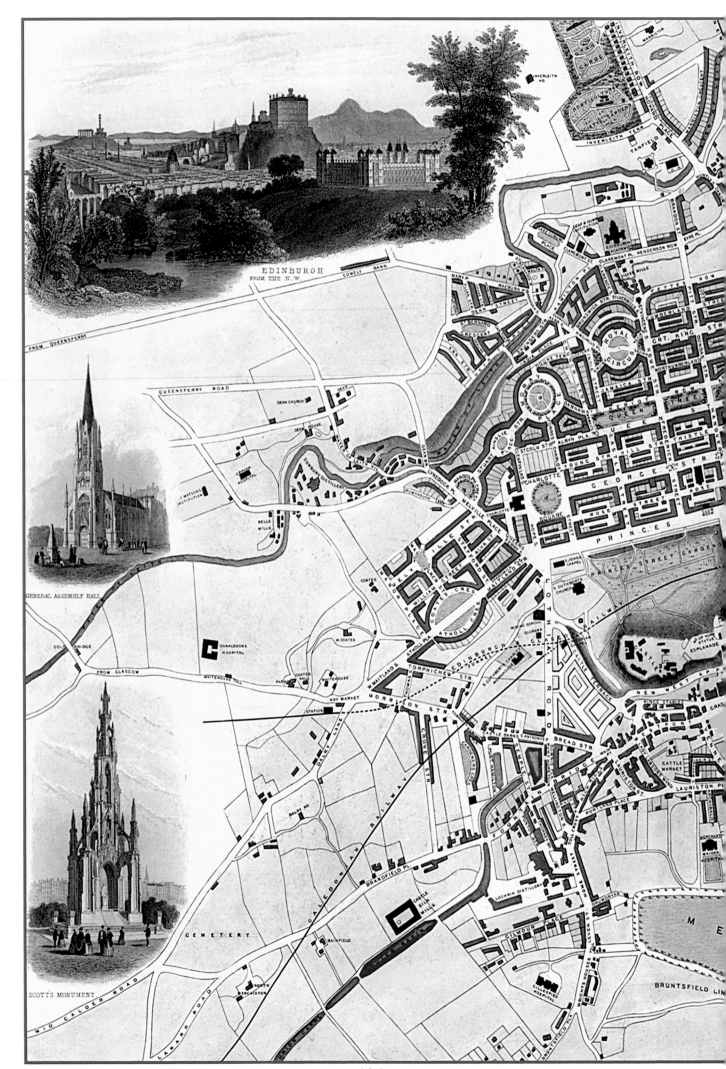

EDINBURGH
FROM THE N.W.

GENERAL ASSEMBLY HALL.

SCOTT'S MONUMENT.

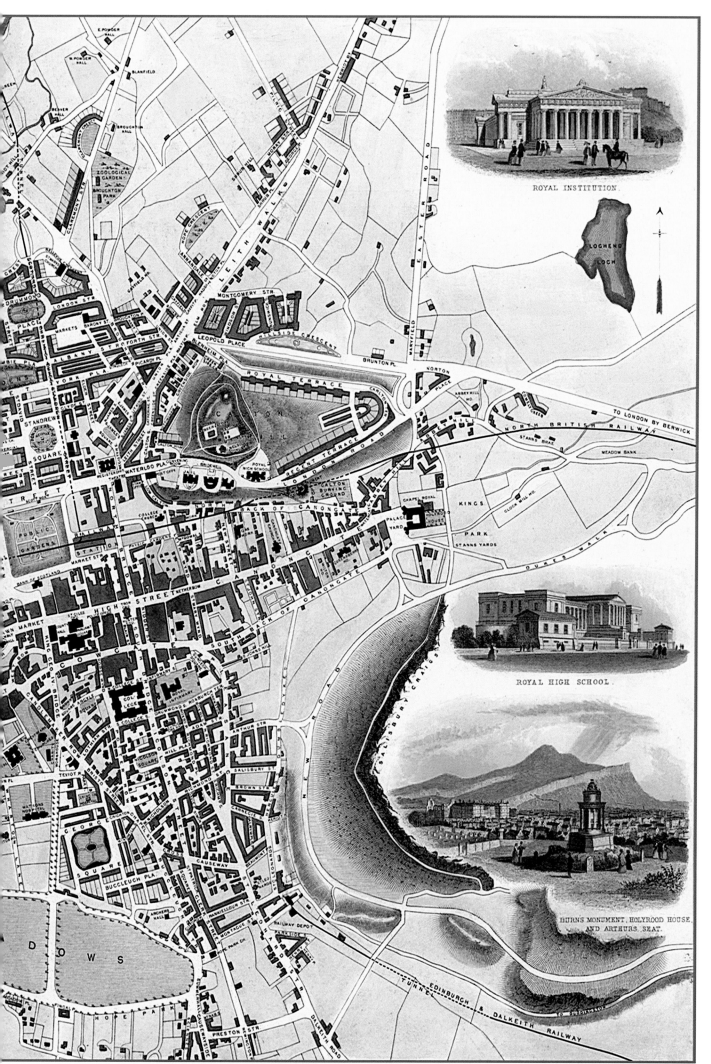

ROYAL INSTITUTION.

LOCHEND LOCH

ROYAL HIGH SCHOOL.

BURNS MONUMENT, HOLYROOD HOUSE,
AND ARTHURS SEAT.

PLATE TEN - EDINBURGH

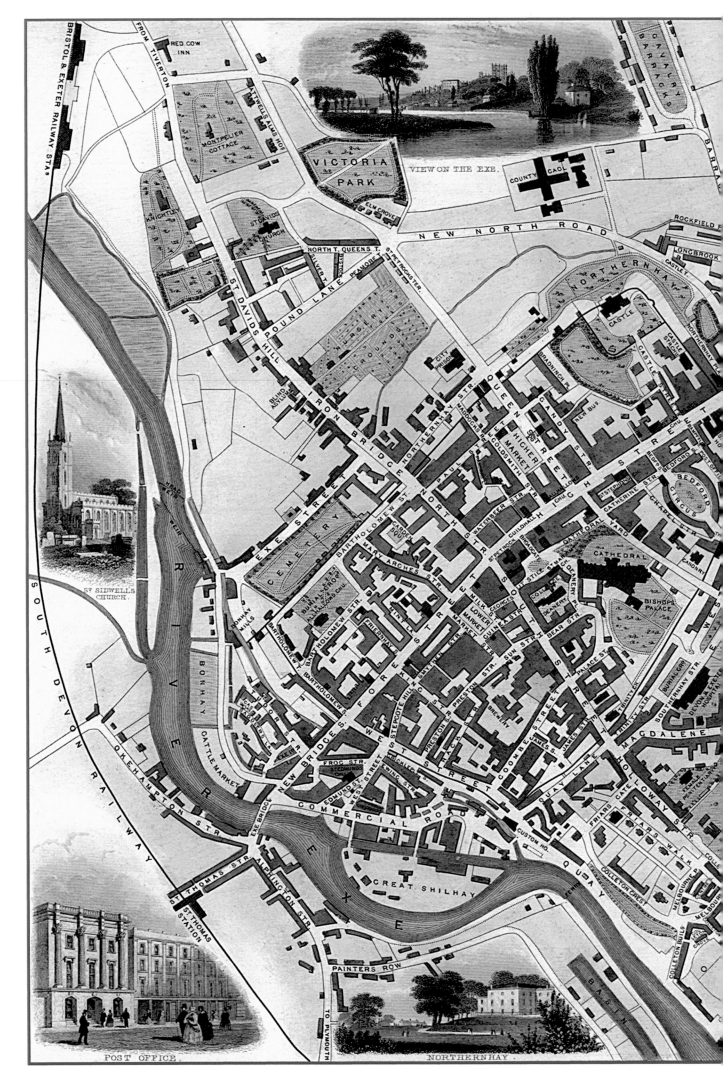

VIEW ON THE EXE.

ST SIDWELLS CHURCH.

POST OFFICE.

NORTHERNHAY.

108

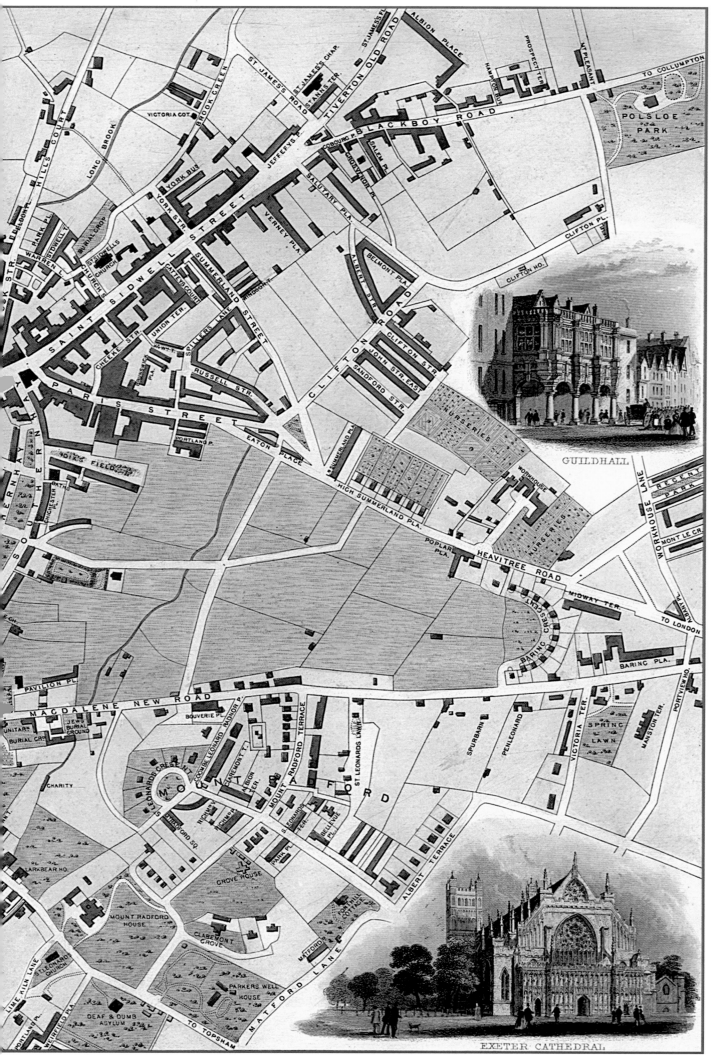

GUILDHALL

EXETER CATHEDRAL

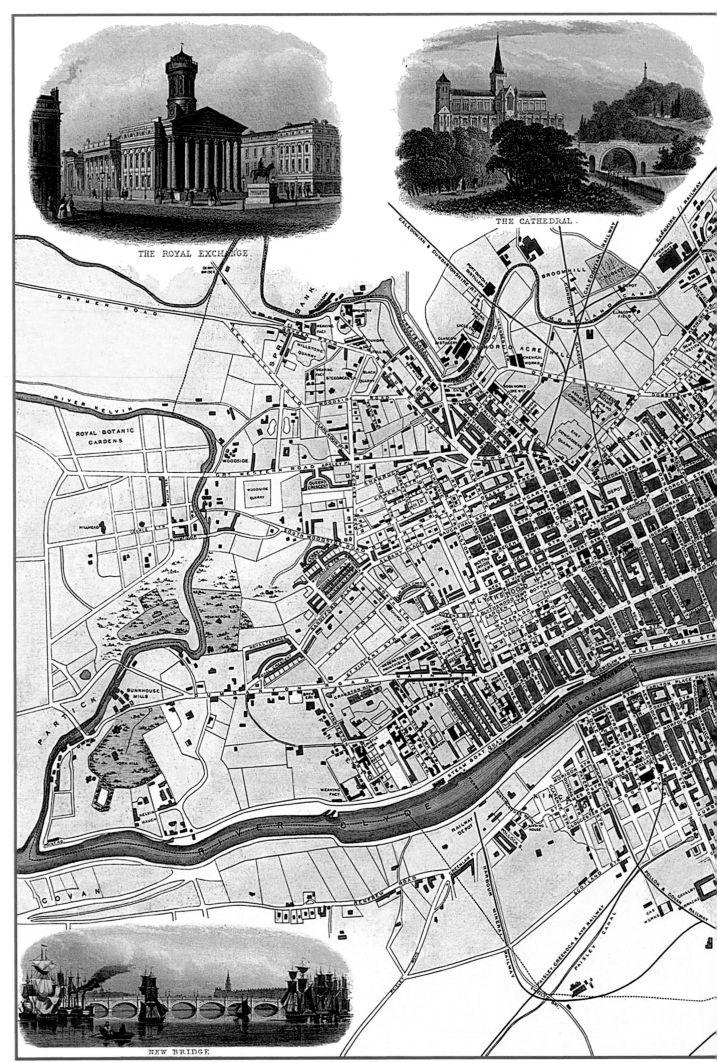

THE ROYAL EXCHANGE.

THE CATHEDRAL.

NEW BRIDGE.

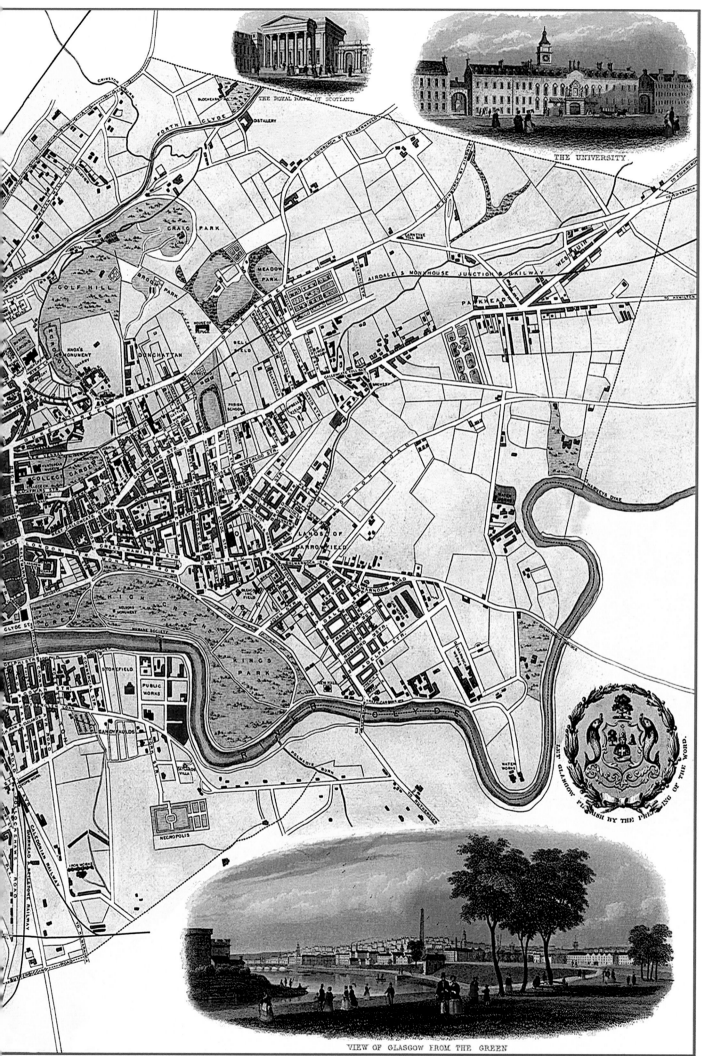

THE ROYAL BANK OF SCOTLAND

THE UNIVERSITY.

VIEW OF GLASGOW FROM THE GREEN

111

PLATE TWELVE - GLASGOW

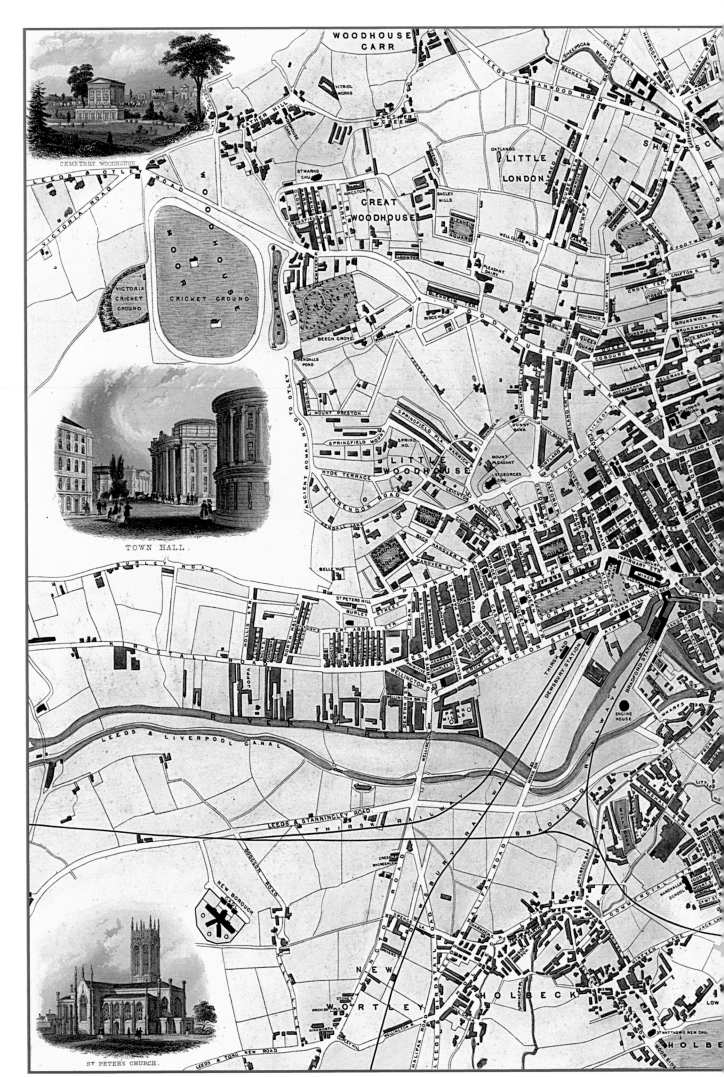

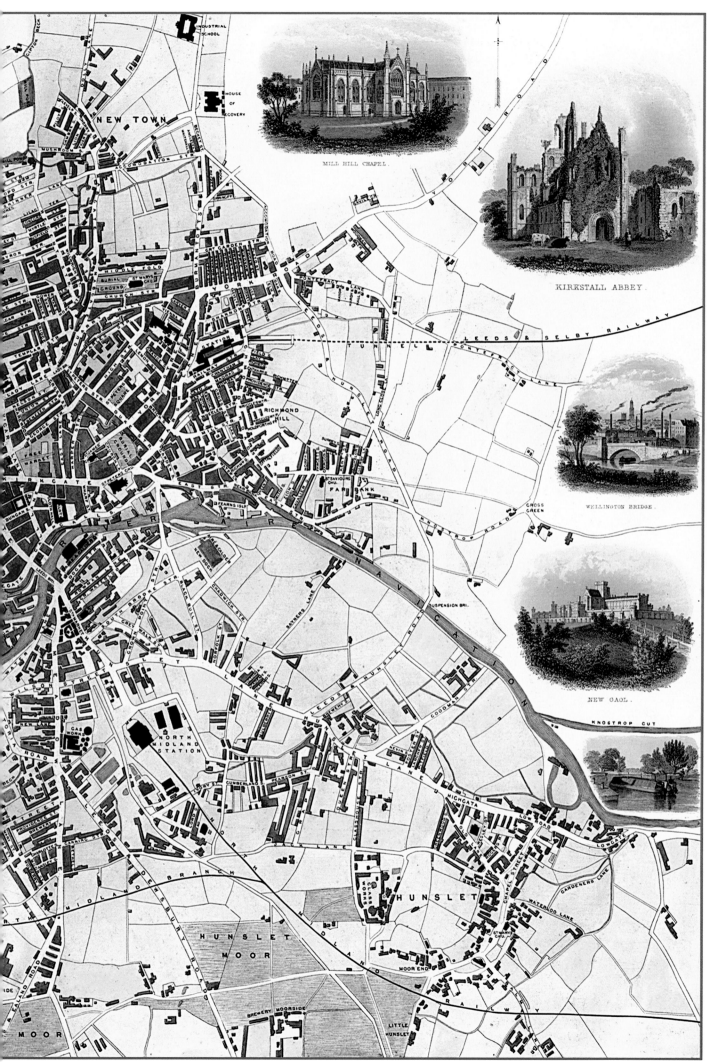

MILL HILL CHAPEL.

KIRKSTALL ABBEY.

WELLINGTON BRIDGE.

NEW GAOL.

KNOSTROP CUT

NEW TOWN

INDUSTRIAL SCHOOL

HOUSE OF RECOVERY

RICHMOND HILL

FAR BANK

CROSS GREEN

LEEDS & SELBY RAILWAY

RIVER AIRE

NAVIGATION

SUSPENSION BRI.

GAS WORKS

NORTH MIDLAND STATION

HUNSLET

HIGHGATE

MOOR END

HUNSLET MOOR

LITTLE HUNSLET

BREWERY MOORSIDE

MOOR

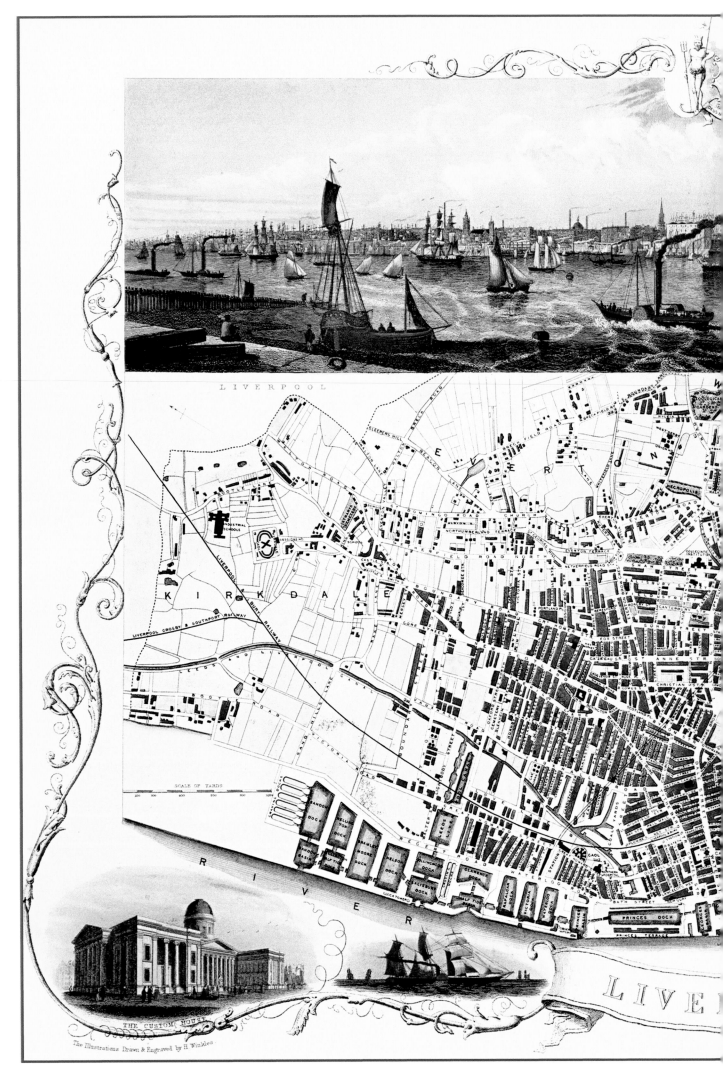

LIVERPOOL

KIRKDALE

EVERTON

SCALE OF YARDS

RIVER

LIVER

THE CUSTOM HOUSE

The Illustrations Drawn & Engraved by H.Winkles.

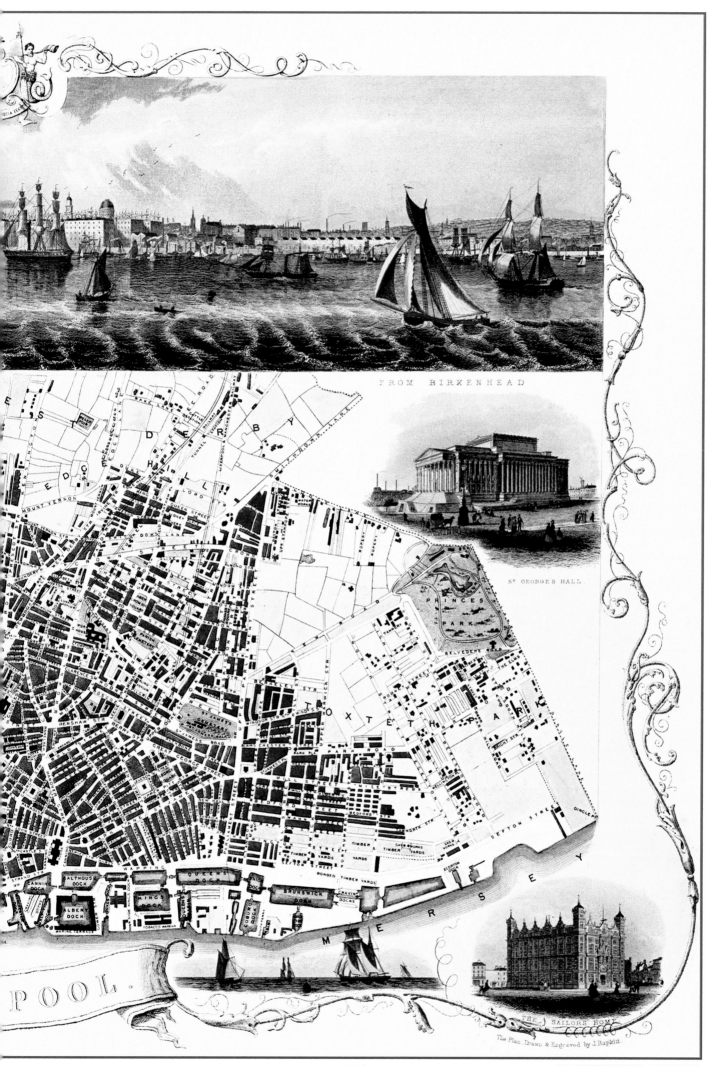

FROM BIRKENHEAD

St GEORGE'S HALL.

THE SAILORS HOME

The Plan Drawn & Engraved by J.Rapkin

PLATE FOURTEEN - LVERPOOL

ROYAL INFIRMARY

BRANCH BANK OF ENGLAND

STRANGEWAYS

COLLEGIATE CHURCH

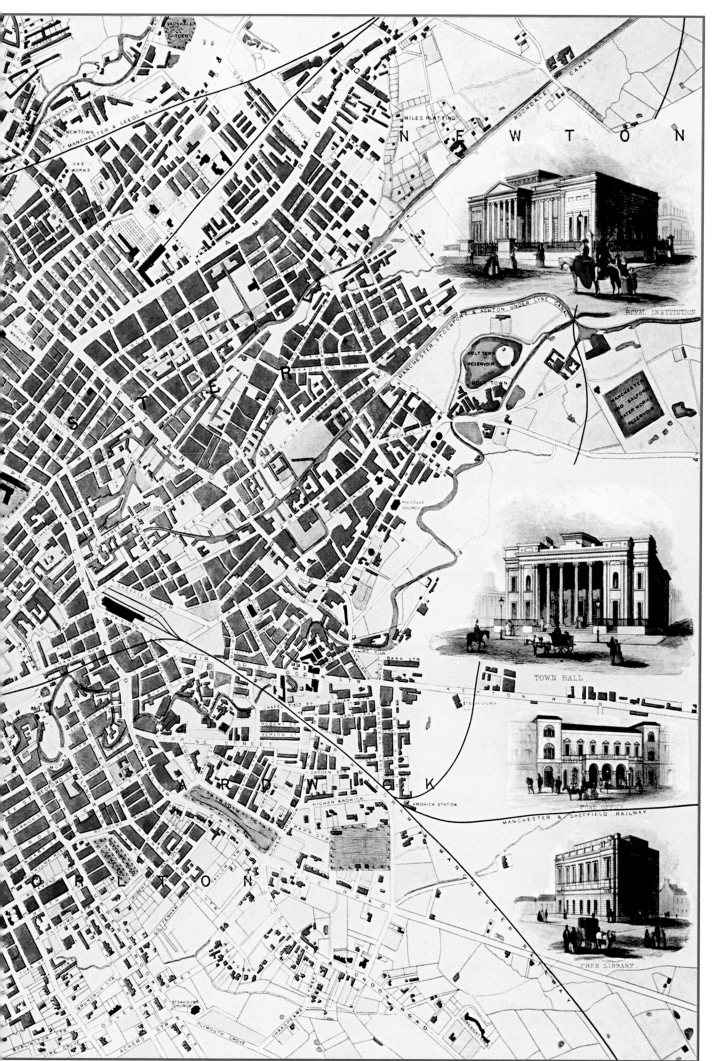

ROYAL INSTITUTION

TOWN HALL

MANCHESTER & SHEFFIELD RAILWAY

FREE LIBRARY

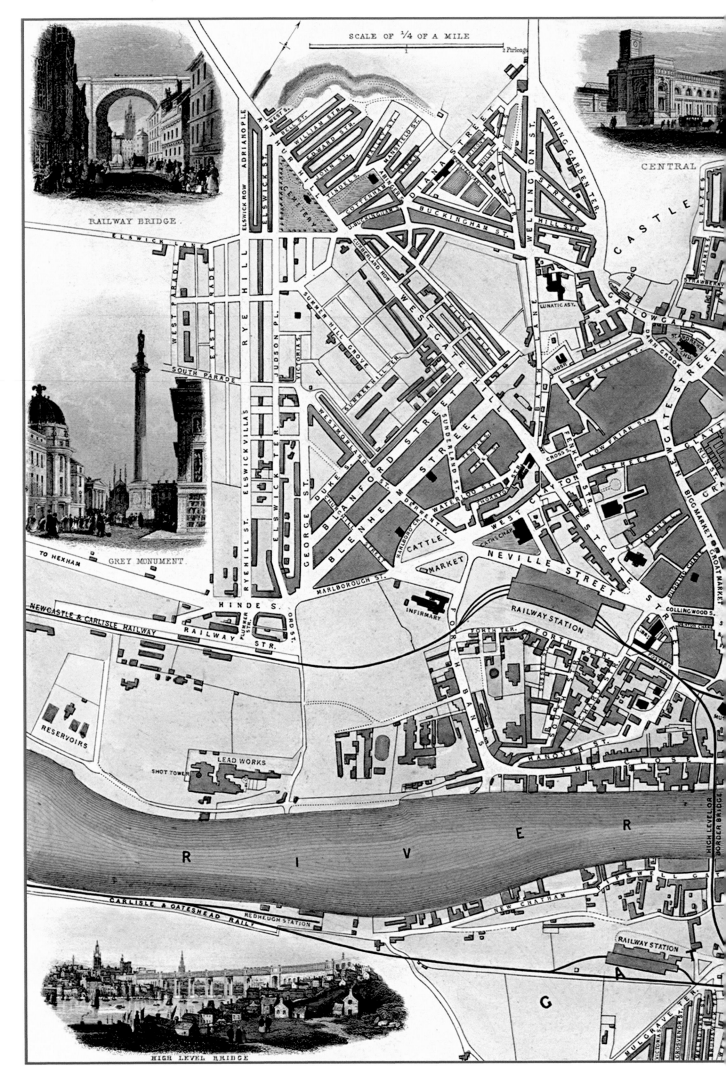

SCALE OF ¼ OF A MILE

RAILWAY BRIDGE.

GREY MONUMENT.

TO HEXHAM

RESERVOIRS

LEAD WORKS

SHOT TOWER

NEWCASTLE & CARLISLE RAILWAY

RAILWAY STR.

PLUMER STR.

HINDE S.

ORD ST.

RYE HILL ST.

WEST PARADE

EAST PARADE

SOUTH PARADE

ELSWICK LA.

ELSWICK ROW

ADRIANOPLE

ARTHUR HILL

ELSWICK ST.

WEST ST.

RYE HILL

JUDSON PL.

ELSWICK VILLAS

ELSWICK TER.

GEORGE ST.

BLENHEIM STREET

WESTMORLAND

MARLBOROUGH ST.

SUMMER HILL GROVE

SUMMER HILL TER.

VICTORIA S.

DUKE ST.

CEMETERY

BELL ST.

WILLIAM STR.

EDWARD STR.

JOHN ST.

TINDLE S.

COTTENHAM

U. BUCKINGHAM

ABIGAIL

TAYLOR ST.

MARSHALL ST.

MARTIN S.

MANSFIELD ST.

BUCKINGHAM ST.

SUNDERLAND ROW

WESTGATE STREET

BLANFORD ST.

SUNDERLAND ST.

WATERLOO S.

DERWENT P.

HULL ST.

MARLBORO CH.

DIANA STREET

WELLINGTON ST.

SPRING GARDEN TER.

HILL STR.

HESTER S.

HOUSTON S.

CATTLE MARKET

CATTLE MARKET

CATH.S CHAP.

INFIRMARY

NEVILLE STREET

RAILWAY STATION

FORTH

LUNATIC AS.Y.

MOSK.

STOVELL ST.

LOW FRIAR ST.

CROSS S.

FENKLE STR.

WEST CLAYTON STREET

CLAY

WEST GATE STR.

PILGRIM CHA.

BIGG MARKET

GROAT MARKET

COLLINGWOOD S.

SIDE

CASTLE

CALLOWGA.

DARN CROOK

STRAWBER.

ST. JOHN ST.

CENTRAL

FORTH TER.

FORTH STR.

PORTH BANKS

SCOTT'S R.D

HANOVER ST.

THE CLOSE

HIGH LEVEL

BORDER BRIDGE

RIVER

CARLISLE & GATESHEAD RAILT.

REDHEUGH STATION

NEW CHATHAM

RAILWAY STATION

POWELL S.

MULGRAVE ST.

CROSVENOR TER.

VICTORIA TER.

G

A

HIGH LEVEL BRIDGE

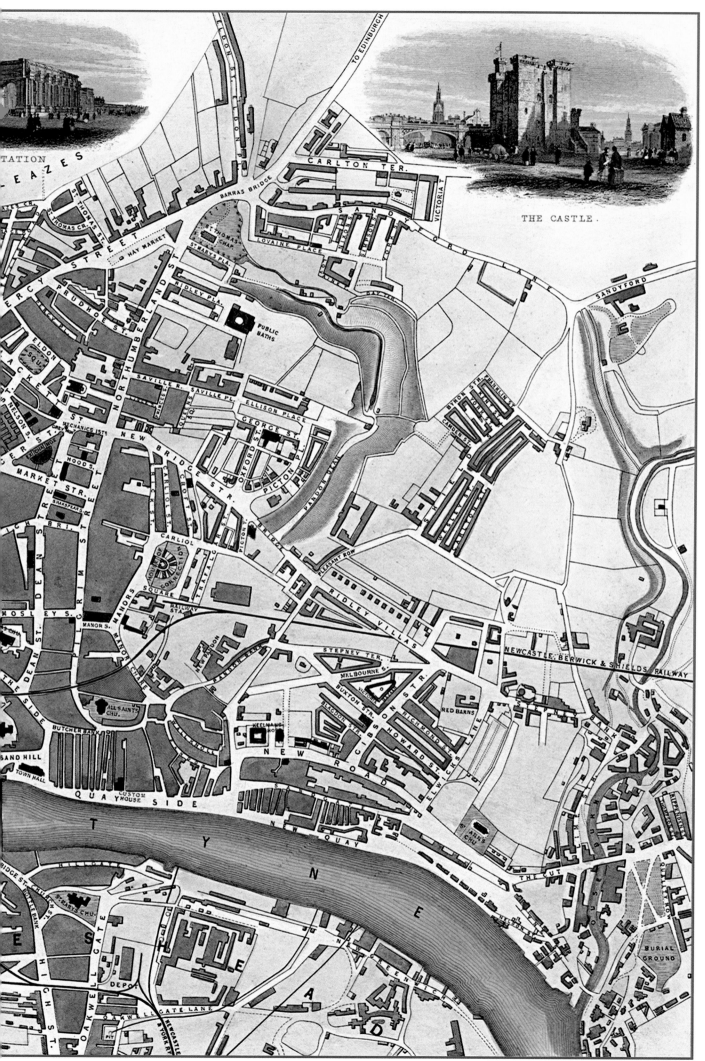

THE CASTLE.

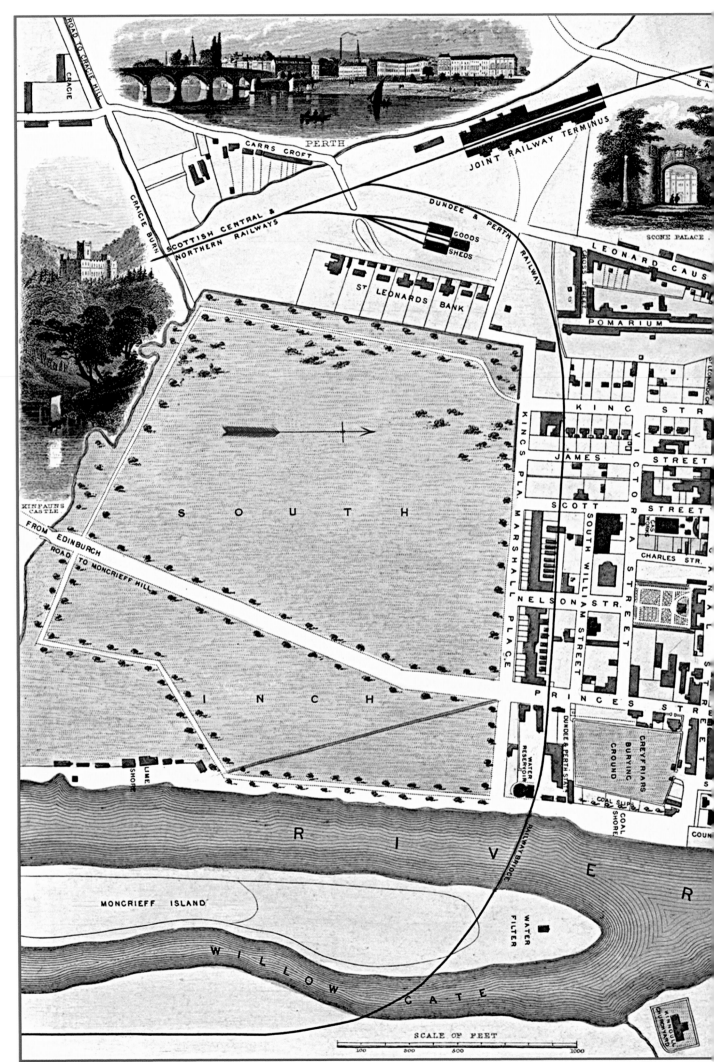

PERTH

ROAD TO CRAIGIE HILL

CRAIGIE

CARRS CROFT

SCOTTISH CENTRAL & NORTHERN RAILWAYS

CRAIGIE BURN

JOINT RAILWAY TERMINUS

DUNDEE & PERTH RAILWAY

GOODS SHEDS

ST LEONARDS BANK

SCONE PALACE

LEONARD CAUS

POMARIUM

CROSS STREET

ST LEONARDS ST

KINFAUNS CASTLE

SOUTH

INCH

FROM EDINBURGH

ROAD TO MONCRIEFF HILL

KINGS PLACE. MARSHALL PLACE

NELSON

PRINCES

STREET

KING STR

JAMES

SCOTT

SOUTH WILLIAM STR.

SOUTH WILLIAM STREET

VICTORIA STREET

VICTORIA

STREET

STREET

CHARLES STR.

GAS WORKS

CANAL STREET

PRINCES STREETS

FLUME SHORE

WATER RESERVOIR

DUNDEE & PERTH STA.

GREYFRIARS BURYING GROUND

COAL SLIP

COAL SHORE

COUN

MONCRIEFF ISLAND

RIVER

WILLOW GATE

RAILWAY BRIDGE

WATER FILTER

KINNOULL CHURCHYARD

SCALE OF FEET

100   300   600   1000

120

PERTH.

BANK OF SCOTLAND.

SCOTTISH MIDLAND RAILWAY

FROM GLASGOW

DYKE

KINNOULL CAUSEWAY

INFIRMARY

YORK PLA.

COUNTY PLACE

NEW ROW

CLAY HOLES

CLAYPOTS WYND

TOWNS AQUADUCT

BARRACKS

BARRACK STR.

LOW STR.

MELVILLE STR.

ATHOLL STREET

STORMONT STR.

BAROSSA STR.

BAROSSA PLACE

BALHOUSIE

CHURCH

ST PAULS

SOUTH METHVEN STR.

NORTH METHVEH STREET

MURRAY STR.

FOUNDRY LANE

WILLIAM STR.

UNION LANE

KINNOULL STR.

ROSE TERRACE

CANAL CRES

HIGH STREET

MEAL VENNEL

MILL STREET

CUTLOG VENNEL

BLACK FRIARS

BLACKFRIARS WYND

CARPENTER STR.

BLACKFRIARS S.

CRESCENT

RACE COURSE

NORTH INCH

SOUTH STREET

NEW CITY HALL

CURFEW ROW

VIEW

NORTH PORT

ATHOLL PLACE

CASTLE CABLE

ST JOHNS CH.

KIRKSIDE

ST JOHNS PL.

KIRKGATE

KIRKGATE

GEORGE STREET

CHARLOTTE S.

ST JOHNS STREET

WATERGATE

GEORGE STREET

BRIDGE

T A Y

BUILDINGS

TO DUNDEE

COMMERCIAL STR.

COWRIE STR.

BACK WYND

BRIDGE STREET

BRIDGE END

TO BLAIRGOWRIE

TO CUPAR

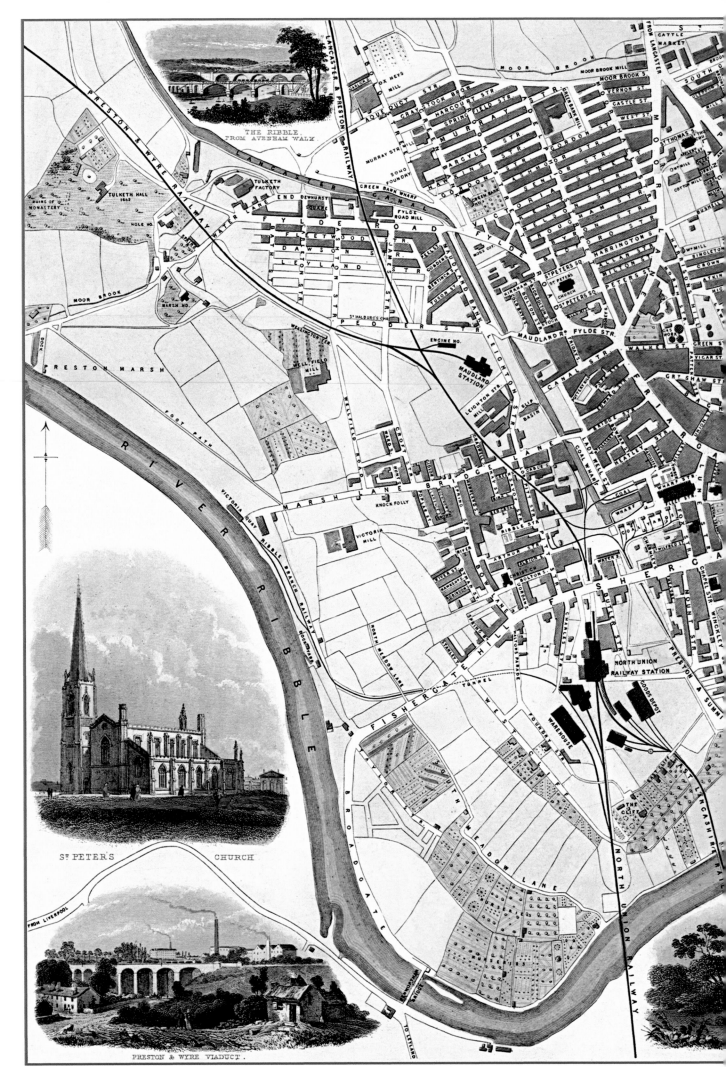

THE RIBBLE,
FROM AVENHAM WALK.

ST PETER'S   CHURCH

PRESTON & WYRE VIADUCT.

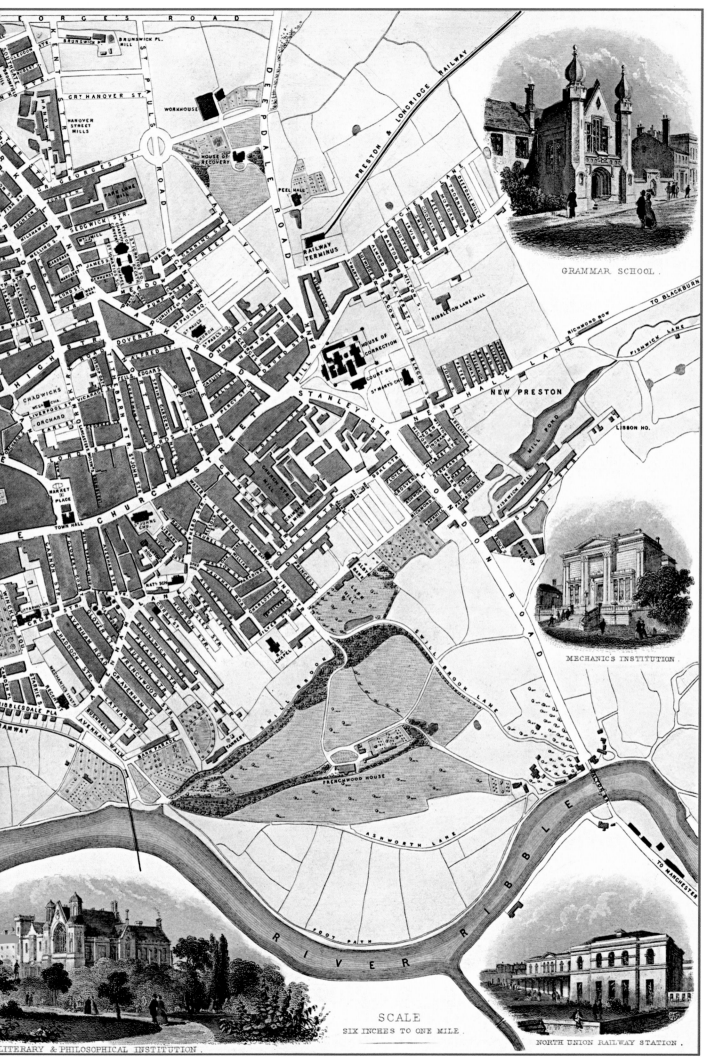

GRAMMAR SCHOOL.

MECHANIC'S INSTITUTION.

LITERARY & PHILOSOPHICAL INSTITUTION.

SCALE
SIX INCHES TO ONE MILE.

NORTH UNION RAILWAY STATION.

SHEFFIELD.
FROM THE SOUTH EAST

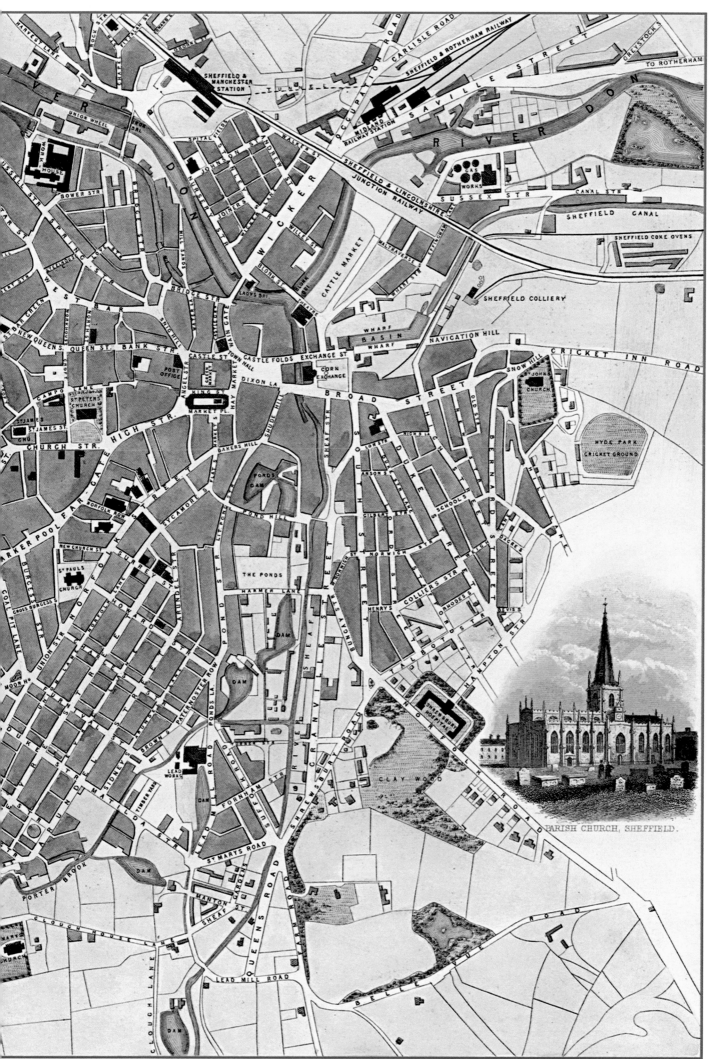

PARISH CHURCH, SHEFFIELD.

PLATE NINETEEN - SHEFFIELD

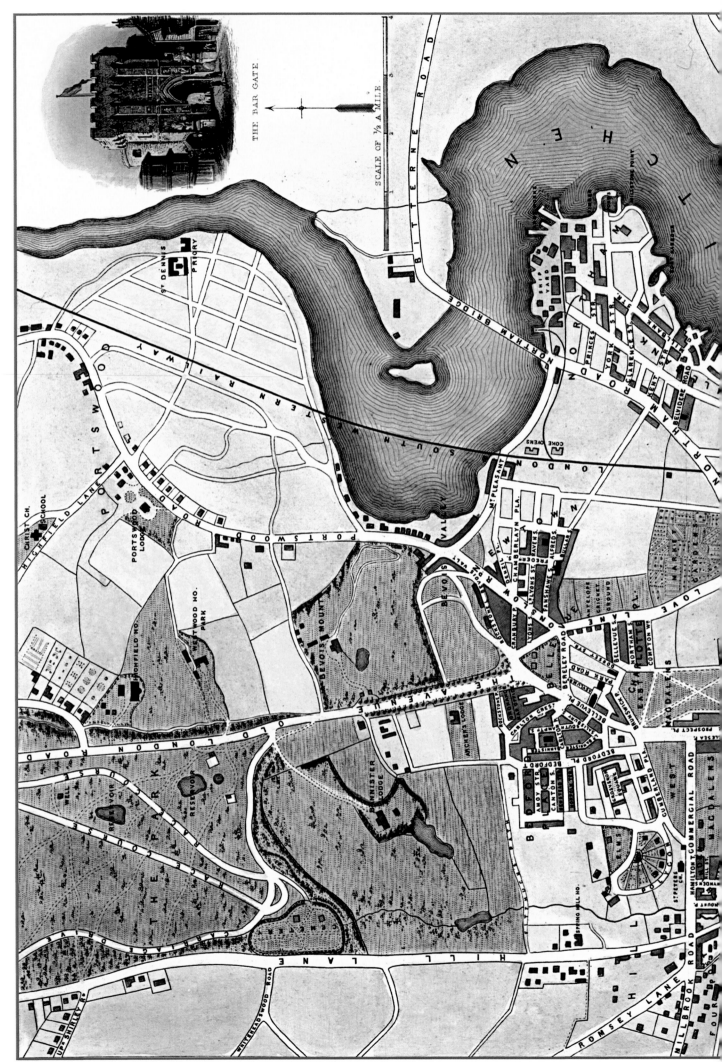

THE BAR GATE.

SCALE OF ½ A MILE

RAILWAY STATION

SOUTHAMPTON.

NETLEY ABBEY.

PLATE TWENTY - SOUTHAMPTON

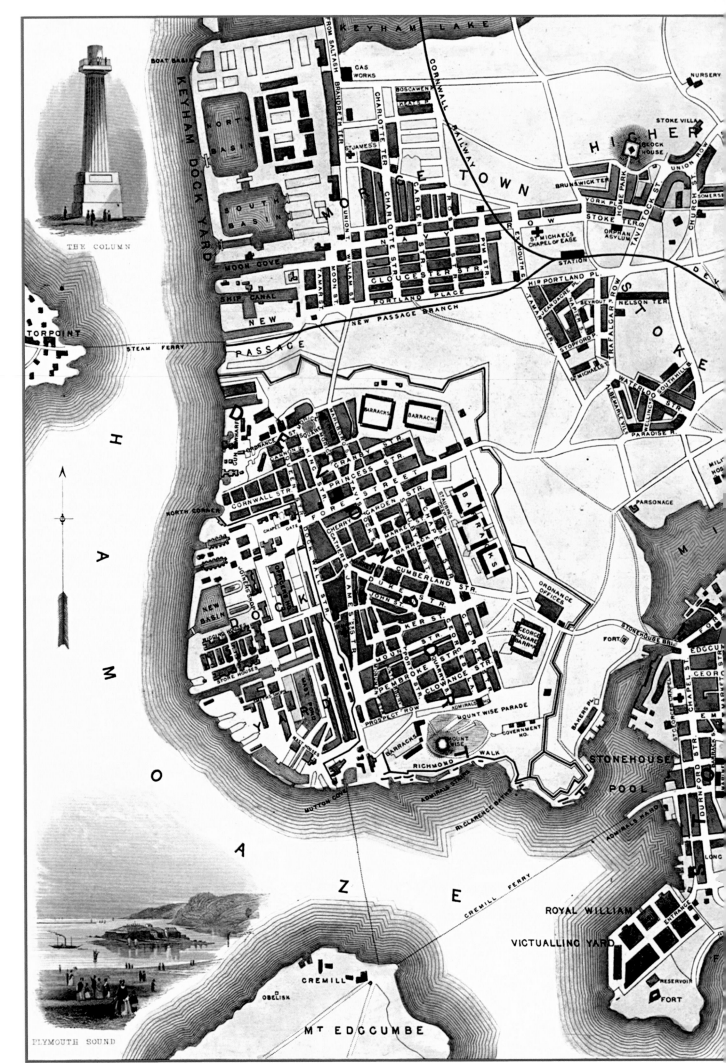

THE COLUMN

TORPOINT

STEAM FERRY

PLYMOUTH SOUND

KEYHAM LAKE

BOAT BASIN

KEYHAM DOCK YARD

NORTH BASIN

SOUTH BASIN

MOON COVE

SHIP CANAL

NEW

GAS WORKS

FROM SALTASH

BRANDRETH TER.

CHARLOTTE TER.

ST JAMES'S

MORICE TOWN

BOSCAWEN PLACE

CORNWALL RAILWAY

HIGHER

STOKE VILLA

NURSERY

CLOCK HOUSE

BRUNSWICK TER.

HOME PARK

YORK PL.

UNION ST.

GARDEN STR.

CHARLOTTE STR.

WILLIAM ST.

MOON ST.

TAMAR ST.

GLOUCESTER STR.

PYM STR.

EXMOUTH STR.

ROW

PORTLAND PLACE

ST MICHAEL'S CHAPEL OF EASE

ORPHAN ASYLUM

STOKE TER.

TAVISTOCK ST.

UNION ST.

CHURCH ST.

SOMERSET

STATION

HIR PORTLAND PL.

JEAN DACRE PL.

NAPIER'S

BEYROUT P.

NELSON TER.

STOKE

TAMAR TER.

STOPFORD P.

TRAFALGAR ROW

NEW PASSAGE BRANCH

PASSAGE

ST MICHAELS

ALBEMARLE VILLAS

WATERLOO

WELLING STR.

SOUTH MILLS

PARADISE R.

BARRACKS

BARRACKS

H A M

O A Z E

NORTH CORNER

CUM SOMMT.

ORDNANCE

POST OFFICE

ST GEORGE SQUARE

CANNON STR.

KING STR.

GRANBY STR.

PRINCESS STR.

FORE STR.

TAVISTOCK STR.

GARDEN STR.

MARKET

CHAPEL STR.

ST AUBINS

BARRACKS

CORNWALL STR.

CHAPEL GATE

CHERRY STR.

CATHER'S

JAMES STR.

DOCK STR.

OCTAGON STR.

CUMBERLAND STR.

BARRACK STR.

PARSONAGE

NEW BASIN

JOINERS SHOP

D O C K Y A R D

OFFICE HA.

DUKE STR.

JOHN ST.

GEORGE STR.

ORDNANCE OFFICES

RIGGING HOUSE

KER ST.

GEORGE STR.

GEORGE SQUARE BARR.

FORT

STONEHOUSE BRI.

EDGCUM

STONE HOUSES

MOUNT ST.

CLOWANCE STR.

CHAPEL ST.

GEORGE ST.

EAST FORD ROAD

YORK STR.

PROSPECT ROW

PEMBROKE STR.

ADMIRALS HARD

MOUNT WISE PARADE

BAKERS PL.

STONEHOUSE

ST GEORGE CHAPEL ST.

DURNFORD STR.

MARKET STR.

BARRACKS

MOUNT WISE

GOVERNMENT HO.

POOL

LONG

MUTTON COVE

RICHMOND WALK

ADMIRALS STAIRS

R. CLARENCE BATH

CREMILL FERRY

ROYAL WILLIAM

ENTRANCE

CREMILL

OBELISK

MT EDGCUMBE

VICTUALLING YARD

RESERVOIR

FORT

128

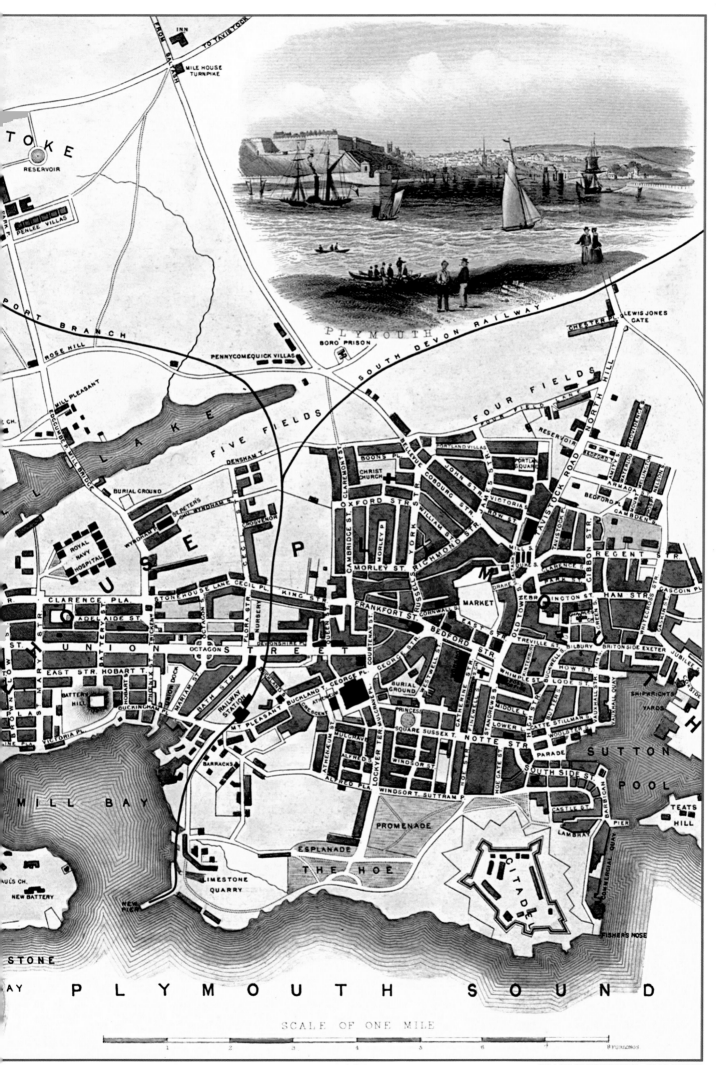

TO TAVISTOCK
INN
FROM SALTASH
MILE HOUSE
TURNPIKE
STOKE
RESERVOIR
PENLEE VILLAS
PORT BRANCH
ROSE HILL
MILL PLEASANT
PENNYCOMEQUICK VILLAS
EDGCUMBE MILL BRIDGE
MILL LAKE
FIVE FIELDS
FOUR FIELDS
NORTH HILL
RESERVOIR
INNER FIELD LANE
PLYMOUTH
BORO' PRISON
SOUTH DEVON RAILWAY
CHESTER PL.
LEWIS JONES GATE
DENSHAM T.
BURIAL GROUND
ST. PETERS CH.
WYNDHAM STR.
WYNDHAM
CECIL
GROSVENOR
CLAREMONT ST.
OXFORD STR.
CHRIST CHURCH
BOONS PL.
BELLEVUE PL.
PORTLAND VILLAS
PORTLAND SQUARE
JOHN STR.
COBOURG STR.
VICTORIA ST.
BEDFORD PL.
ARMADA
CAMDEN
AMITY PL.
WATERLOO
WELLINGTON
HILL'S PL.
ROYAL NAVY HOSPITAL
STONEHOUSE
HOUSE
CAMBRIDGE ST.
MORLEY P.
YORK
WILLIAM STR.
RICHMOND STR.
MORLEY ST.
ROW ST.
REGENT STR.
CASCOIN PL.
CLARENCE PLA.
ADELAIDE ST.
STONEHOUSE LANE
CECIL PL.
KING STR.
FRANKFORT ST.
RUSSELL STR.
CORNWALL STR.
OLD TOWN STR.
ZEBRA ST.
TAVISTOCK PL.
CLARENCE ST.
PARK STR.
GIBBON STR.
HAM STR.
ST. MARY STR.
BATTERY ST.
UNION
FLORA STR.
BURBERY
QUEEN
DEVONSHIRE ST.
MARKET
DRAKE
SQUARE ST.
TREVILLE ST.
BILBURY
BRITON SIDE
EXETER
JUBILEE
COXSIDE
OCTAGON STR.
STREET
COURTENAY ST.
BEDFORD STR.
EAST STR.
WHIMPLE ST.
BUCKWELL LODGE ST.
HOW ST.
HOBART T.
PHOENIX
MARIAM STR.
BATH STR.
GEORGE PL.
GEORGE STR.
CATHERINE STR.
FINEWELL
MIDDLE ST.
HIGH STR.
VAUXHALL QUAY
SHIPWRIGHTS YARDS
EAST STR.
PHOENIX
UNION DOCK
RAILWAY STATION
BUCKLAND T.
ATHENEUM
BURIAL GROUND
ST. ANDREWS S.
CATTE STR.
STILLMAN ST.
WORCESTER
BATTERY HILL
BUCKINGHAM
MT. PLEASANT
CRESCENT
PRINCESS
SUSSEX T.
SQUARE
PARADE
SUTTON
VICTORIA PL.
BARRACKS
ATHENEUM ST.
MULGRAVE PL.
LOCKYER TER.
MULGRAVE ST.
ALFRED ST.
WINDSOR ST.
NOTTE STR.
HOE GATE ST.
LOWER STR.
SOUTH SIDE ST.
CASTLE ST.
BARBICAN
POOL
MILL BAY
ALFRED PLA.
WINDSOR T.
SUTTRAM P.
PROMENADE
LAMBHAY
PIER
TEATS HILL
ESPLANADE
THE HOE
LIMESTONE QUARRY
CITADEL
COMMERCIAL QUAY
PAUL'S CH.
NEW BATTERY
NEW PIER
FISHER'S NOSE
STONE
BAY
PLYMOUTH SOUND

SCALE OF ONE MILE

1   2   3   4   5   6   7   8 FURLONGS

PLATE TWENTY ONE - PLYMOUTH

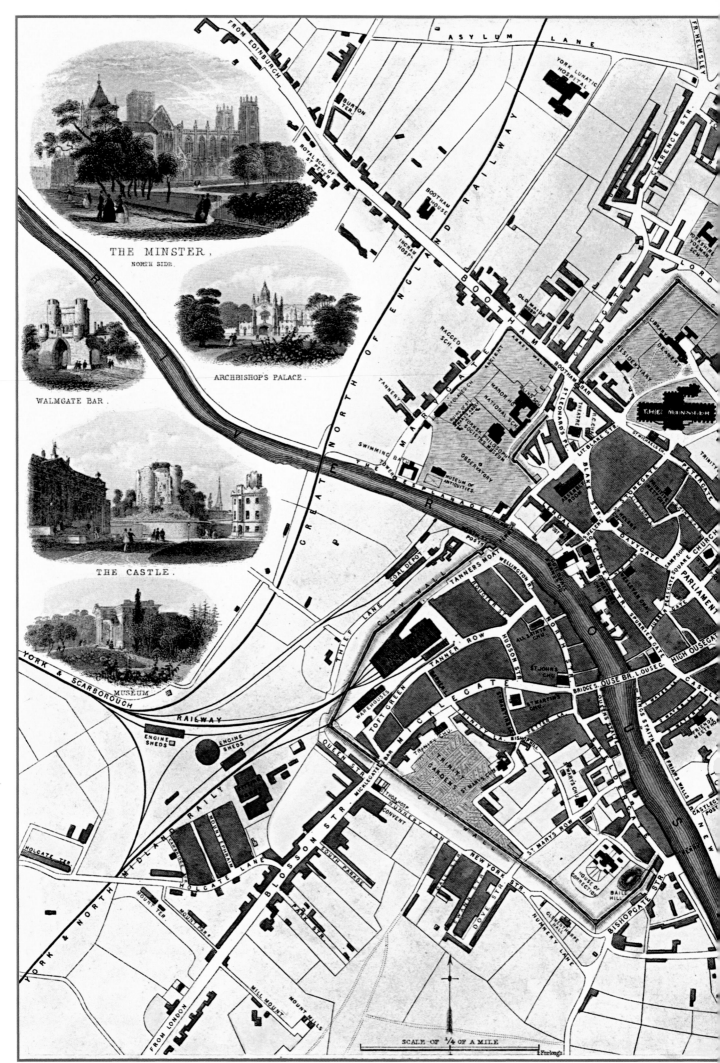

THE MINSTER,
NORTH SIDE.

WALMGATE BAR.

ARCHBISHOP'S PALACE.

THE CASTLE.

MUSEUM.

SCALE OF ¼ OF A MILE

1 Furlong.

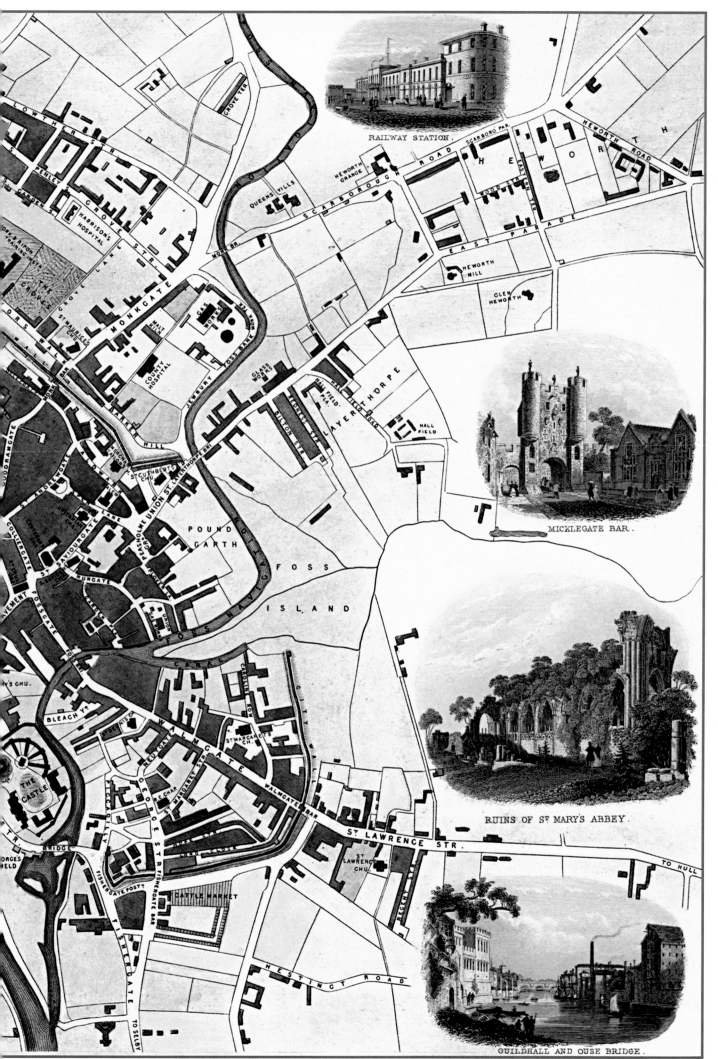

RAILWAY STATION.

MICKLEGATE BAR.

RUINS OF ST. MARY'S ABBEY.

GUILDHALL AND OUSE BRIDGE.

SOUTH WESTERN RAILWAY STATION - NINE ELMS

BRIGHTON RAILWAY STATION - LONDON BRIDGE

Four

INDEX TO RAILWAY STATIONS
GREAT BRITAIN AND IRELAND 1852

The index that follows contains an alphabetical list of as many of the railway stations and destinations as possible given that not all were legible enough to be read on the original Bradshaw map of Great Britain and Ireland 1852. These are recorded in the first column of page numbers. The second column shows the page number in the Bradshaw's Guide of 1866 where a reference to the station or place can be found (no entry means no reference could be determined). During the process of building the index some discrepancies were found between entries on the map and those corresponding in the guide book. This is mainly due to either incorrect spelling at the time of producing the original or a change of name between 1852 and 1866. Where spelling differences were found, the entry on the map was not changed so as to replicate the original railway map exactly as it was produced in 1852. Some stations closed between 1852 and when the guide book was originally produced in 1866, however this was dwarfed by the number of stations opened on new railway lines in the same period. This small deficiency aside, the index still acts as a wonderful reference to the many railway stations and destinations, relating them back to the informative textual content contained within the guide book. Those entries in red are recorded on the original 1852 map as principal stations and locations, those in green are contained within Ireland.

Also included in the index section are two railway maps – one of Lancashire and another of central England - from an original copy of Bradshaw's Railway Companion dated February 1841, the forerunner to the Railway Guide first published in December 1841. Along with these maps, the incredible growth of the railways in just over 10 years can be seen by referring to the table on page 142, numerically referenced back to George Bradshaw's railway map of England and Wales 1841, featured on page 68.

SOUTHAMPTON RAILWAY TERMINUS

STATIONS	ATLAS	GUIDE
ABBEY	27	317
ABBEY WOOD	44	38
ABER	30	204
ABERDEEN	21	351
ABERGELE	30	202
ABERNETHY	20	341
ABINGDON	43	131
ABINGTON	24	327
ARBROATH	21	345
ACKLINGTON	25	466
ACTON	31	285
ADLINGTON	31	305
ADLINGTON	36	281
AINSDALE	31	305
AINTREE	31	436
AIRDRIE	23	336
ALBRIGHTON	42	189
ALDERLEY	31	288
ALDERMASTON	49	129
ALFORD	37	424
ALGARKIRK	37	422
ALNE	28	80
ALNWICK	25	467
ALSAGER	31	279
ALTON	36	280
ALTON	49	91
ALTRINGHAM	31	198
AMBER GATE	36	387
AMPTHILL	43	260
ANDOVER RD	49	92
ANDOVER	49	92
ANGMERING	49	76
ANNAN	27	319
ANTRIM	57	236
ARDLEIGH	45	412
ARDLER	20	348
ARDROSSAN	23	322
ARMAGH	56	232
ARMITAGE	36	276
ARUNDEL	49	68
ASHCHURCH	42	183
ASH	49	47
ASHFORD	44	83
ASHFORD	50	54
ASHTON	31	428
ASHWELL	37	378
ASKERN	36	427
ASTLEY	31	197
ASPATRIA	27	310
ATHENRY	59	225
ATHERSTONE	43	274
ATHERTON	31	303
ATHLONE	60	225
ATHY	60	212
ATTLEBORO	44	407
AUCHENGRAY	24	328
AUCHINLECK	23	321
AUCHTERARDER	20	343
AUDLEY END	44	399
AULDBAR ROAD	20	349
AUTHORPE	37	424
AYCLIFFE	28	461
AYLESBURY	43	258
AYNHO	43	135
AYR	27	322
AYTON	25	469
BAGILLT	31	201
BAGNALSTOWN	64	212
BALBRIGGAN	61	229
BALCOMBE	49	70
BALDERSBY	28	456
BALDOYLE & SUTTON	55	228
BALLINASLOE	60	225
BALLINHASSIG	67	219
BALLYMENA	57	237
BALLYNURE	57	236
BALLYPALLADY	57	
BAMBER BRIDGE	31	436
BANBURY	43	179
BANDON	67	219
BANGOR	30	204
BANNOCKBURN	23	330
BANSHA	63	
BANWELL	47	146
BARDNEY	37	423
BARDON MILL	28	318
BARNET	44	418
BARNETBY	37	432
BARNSLEY	36	429
BARNSTAPLE	47	152
BARNEWELL	43	265
BARRHEAD	23	336
BARROW	36	306
BARTON	29	107
BARTON (MOSS)	31	294
BARTON & WALTON	36	384
BASCHURCH	31	191
BASFORD	36	381
BASFORD	31	283
BASINGSTOKE	49	92
BATH	48	142
BATLEY	36	395
BAWTRY	36	427
BAY HORSE	27	310
BEAL	25	467
BEATTOCK	24	327
BEAUGARC	61	
BEAULIEU RD.	48	
BEBINGTON	31	197
BEDALE	28	456
BEDFORD	43	260
BEESTON	31	284
BEITH	23	325
BELFAST	57	233
BELFORD	25	467
BELL BUSK	28	395
BELMONT	28	
BELPER	36	387
BEMPTON	29	445
BENNETT'S BRIDGE	64	213
BENTHAM	28	
BENTLEY JUNCTION	45	412
BERKELEY	42	387
BERKAMPSTEAD	43	257
BERWICK	25	467
BERWICK	50	71
BEVERLY	29	444
BEXHILL	50	72
BICESTER	43	261
BIGGLESWADE	44	419
BILLING RD.	43	265
BILLINGHAM	28	457
BILNEY	37	406
BINGLEY	28	395
BIRKDALE (STATION)	31	305
BIRKENHEAD	31	197
BIRMINGHAM	42	271
BISHOP AUCKLAND	28	460
BISHOP BRIGGS	23	336
BISHOPS STORTFORD	44	399
BISHOPSTOKE JUNCTION	49	94
BLACKBURN	31	436
BLACKFORD	20	343
BLACKPOOL	31	305
BLACKROCK	55	209
BLACKWATER	49	47
BLACKWELL	42	385
BLAIRGOWRIE	20	348
BLANDFORD WIMBORNE	48	109
BLARNEY	63	217
BLAYDON	28	319
BLETCHLEY JUNC.	43	259
BETCHWORTH	49	46
BLISWORTH JUNCTION	43	263
BLUE PITS JUNCTION	36	437
BLYTH BRIDGE	36	277
BLYTON	37	432
BODORGAN	30	208
BOGNOR	49	77
BOHER	63	216
BOLTON	31	311
BOLTON LE MOORS	31	302
BOOTLE	27	307
BOOTERSTOWN	55	209
BORO BRIDGE	28	
BORROWASH	36	384
BOSHAM	49	78
BOSTON	37	422
BOWLAND BRIDGE	24	475
BOX	48	142
BOX HILL	49	46
BOXMOOR	43	256
BRADFORD	36	394
BRAIDWOOD	23	329
BRAINTREE	44	410
BRAMFORD	45	414
BRANDON	44	406
BRAYSTONES	27	307
BRAYTON	27	310
BRECHIN	21	349
BREDON	42	386
BRENT	47	156
BRENTWOOD	44	409
BRIDGEND	41	173
BRIDGE OF ALLAN	20	342
BRIDGE OF DUN J	21	349
BRIDGE OF EARN	20	341
BRIDGEWATER	47	147
BRIDLINGTON	29	445
BRIGG	37	432
BRIGHAM	27	308
BRIGHOUSE	36	440
BRIGHTON	49	72
BRIMSCOMBE	42	137
BRISCO	27	
BRISTOL	42	144
BROCK	27	310
BROCKENHURST	48	108
BROCKLESBY	37	432
BROCKLEY WHINS	28	462
BROMBOROUGH	31	197
BROMFIELD	42	171
BROMSGROVE	42	385
BROMSHALL	36	
BROOKSBY	36	378
BROUGH	37	442
BROUGHTON	27	313
BROUGHTON	31	310
BROUGHTON ASTLEY	43	376
BROUGHTON CROSS	27	308
BROUGHTY FERRY	21	341
BROWNHILLS	36	189
BROXBOURNE	44	398
BRUNDALL	38	408
BUBWITH	29	441
BUCKENHAM	38	408
BULKINGTON	43	274
BULL GILL	27	310
BULWELL	36	381
BURNTISLAND	24	338
BURES	44	411
BURGESS HILL	49	72
BURGH	37	423
BURNBY	29	449
BURNESIDE	27	312
BURNHAM	47	147
BURNLEY	31	435
BURNT MILL	44	399
BURSCOUGH	31	436
BURSLEM	31	279
BURSTON	45	414
BURTON AGNES	29	445
BURTON JOYCE	36	382
BURTON SALMON	36	441
BURY	31	434
BURY LANE	31	197
BURY ST. EDMONDS	44	402
BUSBY	23	336
BUSHEY	43	255
BUTTEVANT	63	217
CAERWEN	30	
CAHER	64	
CALSAGE	63	

Place			Place			Place		
CALVELEY	31	284	CLONMEL	64	214	DITCHFORD	43	265
CAMBRIDGE	44	400	CLONSILLA	61	224	DOGDYKE	37	423
CAMERTON	27	308	CLONTARF	54	228	DONABATE	61	229
CAMPSIE	23	336	CLOSEBURN	23	320	DONCASTER	36	427
CAMPSIE JUNCTION	23	336	COCHRANE MILL	23	325	DONNINGTON	31	282
CANTERBURY	50	55	COCKBURNSPATH	24	470	DORCHESTER	48	111
CAPEL	44	413	COCKERMOUTH	27	308	DORKING	49	46
CARDENDEN	24	339	CODSAL	42	189	DORNOCK	27	
CARDIFF	41	172	COLCHESTER	45	411	DORRINGTON	51	171
CARGILL	20	348	COLD ROWLEY	28	460	DOVER	51	61
CARLISLE	27	316	COLDBLOW & LUCAN	61		DOWNHAM	37	404
CARLOW	64	212	COLERAINE	56	113	DRAYTON	49	77
CARLTON	36	382	COLESHILL	43	385	DREM	24	471
CARLUKE	23	329	COLESWORTH	36		DRIGG	27	307
CARMARTHEN	41	175	COLLESSIE	20	341	DROGHEDA	61	229
CARNABY	29	445	COLLINGHAM	36	382	DROITWICH	42	185
CARNARVON	30	206	COLLISTON	21	346	DROMKEEN	63	216
CARNFORTH	27	311	COLLUMPTON	47	150	DRUMLITHIE	21	350
CARHAM	25	468	COLWICH	36	276	DRUMSOUGH JUNC.	57	
CARNOUSTIE	21	345	COLWYN	30	203	DUBLIN	61	209
CARNWATH	24	328	CONDOVER	31	171	DUBTON JUNCTION	21	349
CARRICK	64		CONGLETON	31	279	DUDLEY	42	188
CARRICKFERGUS	57	235	CONWAY	30	203	DUFFIELD	36	387
CARRICKFERGUS JUNCTION	57	235	COOPER BR.	36		DUHFORD	36	
CARRICKMORE	56	232	COPPULL	31	287	DULEOK	61	
CARRIGANS	56	238	CORBRIDGE	28	318	DULLINGHAM	44	401
CARSTAIRS JUNCTION	24	328	CORK	63	218	DUMFRIES	24	319
CASHEL	63	216	CORNHALL	25	468	DUNADRY	57	236
CASTLE ASHBY	43	265	CORSHAM	42	142	DUNBAR	24	470
CASTLE BROMWICH	42	385	COSHAM	49	97	DUNBLANE	20	342
CASTLECARY	23	337	COUNTESTHORPE	43	376	DUNBRIDGE	48	95
CASTLE EDEN	28	461	COUPAR ANGUS	20	348	DUNDALK	61	230
CASTLE HOWARD	29	450	COVE	21	351	DUNDEE	20	344
CASTLEBLANEY	60	239	COWDENBEATH	24	339	DUNDRUM	63	216
CASTLETOWN	60	225	COXHOLE	28	458	DUNFERMLINE	24	339
CASTOR	43	265	CRAVEN ARMS	42	171	DUNFORD BRIDGE	36	429
CATON	27	396	CRAWLEY BRIDGES	49	68	DUNHAMPSTEAD	42	
CAYTON	29	445	CREDITON	47	152	DUNKELD ROAD	20	346
CELBRIDGE & HAZLEBATCH	61		CRESSWELL	36	277	DUNKELD	20	346
CHANDLERSFORD	49	94	CREWE	31	283	DUNKITT	64	
CHAPEL TOWN	31	302	CRICK	43	266	DUNLEER	61	230
CHARFIELD	42	387	CRIEF JUNCTION	20	343	DUNMURRY	57	233
CHARLEVILLE	63	217	CROBOWEN	31		DUNNING	20	343
CHARLTON	44	36	CROFT	28	459	DUNSTABLE	43	259
CHAT HILL	25	467	CROMFORD	36	388	DURHAM	28	461
CHATTERIS	44	403	CROOK	28	460	EAST FARLEIGH	50	53
CHEADLE	31	428	CROPREDY	43	179	EAST GRINSTEAD	49	69
CHEAM	49	66	CROSBY	31	304	EAST HAVEN	21	345
CHEDDINGTON J	43	257	CROSSGATES	24	339	EASTVILLE	37	423
CHEDDLETON	36	280	CROSTON	31	436	EAST WINCH	37	406
CHELFORD	31	288	CROY	23	337	EASTREA	44	404
CHELMSFORD	44	409	CROYDON	49	66	EASTRINGTON	36	442
CHELTENHAM	42	138	CULLOVILLE	60	239	ECCLEFECHAN	24	326
CHEPSTOW	42	166	CUMMERTREES	27	319	ECCLES	31	293
CHERTSEY	49	89	CUMNOCK	23		ECCLES ROAD	44	407
CHESHUNT	44	398	CUPAR	20	340	ECKINGTON	36	392
CHESTER	31	196	CURRIE	24	328	ECKINGTON	42	386
CHESTERFIELD	36	391	CURTHWAITE	27	310	EDINBRIDGE	50	48
CHESTERFORD	44	399	DAIRSIE	20	340	EDINBURGH	24	476
CHICHESTER	49	77	DALHOUSIE	24	475	EDGE HILL STATION	79	295
CHILHAM	50	55	DALKEITH	24	476	EDMONTON	44	397
CHILWORTH	49	46	DALKEY	55	209	ELLAND	36	440
CHIPPERNHAM	42	139	DALRY	23	312	ELMHAM	38	407
CHIRK	31	193	DALSTON	27	310	ELMSWELL	44	402
CHITTISHAM	44	404	DALTON	27	306	ELSENHAM	44	399
CHURCH FENTON	28	445	DALTON JUNCTION	28	458	ELTON	43	265
CHRISTCHURCH RD	48	109	DARLEY	36	389	ELVANFOOT	24	327
CHRISTON BANK	25	467	DARLINGTON	28	459	ELY	44	403
CHURCH STRETTON	42	171	DARNAL	36	431	EMNETH	37	403
CIRENCESTER	42	136	DARTFORD	44	38	EMSWORTH	49	78
CLAPHAM	28	87	DATCHET	43	83	ENFIELD	60	397
CLAY CROSS	36	391	DAWLISH	47	153	ENNISKILLEN	56	239
CLAYDON	45	261	DEAL	51	57	ENTWISTLE	31	302
CLAYTHORPE	37	424	DEAN	48	95	EPSOM	49	66
CLEVE	42	386	DEEP CAR.	36	430	ERITH	44	38
CLEVEDON	47	146	DEFFORD	42	386	ERRAL	20	344
CLIFF	36	441	DENVER	37	404	ESHER	49	89
CLIFTON	27	315	DERBY	36	384	ESKMEALS	27	307
CLIFTON	31	302	DEREHAM	38	407	ETRURIA	31	278
CLOCKSBRIGGS	20	349	DERWENT HAUGH	28	465	EWELL	49	66
CLONDALKIN	61		DIDCOT JUNC.	43	131	EWOOD BRIDGE	31	434
			DISS	45	414	EXETER	47	150

BRADSHAW'S
Railway Companion,

CONTAINING

THE TIMES OF DEPARTURE,

FARES, &c.

OF THE RAILWAYS IN ENGLAND,

AND ALSO

Hackney Coach Fares

FROM THE PRINCIPAL RAILWAY STATIONS,

ILLUSTRATED WITH

MAPS OF THE COUNTRY THROUGH WHICH THE RAILWAYS PASS,

AND PLANS OF

LONDON, BIRMINGHAM, LEEDS.

LIVERPOOL, AND MANCHESTER.

PRICE ONE SHILLING.

MANCHESTER:

PRINTED & PUBLISHED BY BRADSHAW & BLACKLOCK
27, BROWN-STREET; AND SOLD BY

SHEPHERD & SUTTON, PRIEST COURT, FOSTER LANE
CHEAPSIDE, LONDON;

AND ALL BOOKSELLERS AND RAILWAY COMPANIES

1841.

Station		
EXMOUTH	47	151
FAKENHAM	38	407
FALKIRK	24	337
FALKLAND	24	340
FALMER	50	75
FANGOSS	29	449
FAREHAM	49	96
FARNBOROUGH	49	91
FARNELL R.	21	349
FARRINGDON RD.	43	135
FAY GATE	49	68
FELTHAM	44	83
FENCE HOUSES	28	462
FENNY COMPTON	43	179
FERNS LOCK	60	224
FERRIBY	37	442
FERRY HILL	28	458
FERRY PORT ON CRAIG	21	341
FIDDOWN	64	
FILEY	29	445
FINNINGHAM	45	414
FIRSBY	37	423
FISKERTON	36	382
FIVE MILE HO.	37	
FLAXTON	29	450
FLEETPOND	49	92
FLEETWOOD	27	305
FLINT	31	200
FLORDON	38	415
FOLKESTONE	50	61
FORDOUN	21	350
FOREST GATE	44	409
FORFAR	20	349
FORGANDENNY	20	343
FORMBY	31	304
FORNCETT	38	414
FORTEVIOT	20	343
FOUNTAINHALL	24	475
FOUR ASHES	31	274
FOURSTONES	25	318
FRANSHAM	38	406
FRIOCKHEIM JUNCTION	21	346
FRISBY	36	378
FROCESTER	42	386
FROGHALL	36	280
FRUSTERLEY	28	
FURNESS	27	
GAINSBOROUGH	36	432
GALASHIELS	24	474
GALGATE	27	310
GALSTON	23	321
GALWAY	59	225
GANTON	29	451
GARGRAVE	28	395
GARSTANG	27	310
GATE HERNSLEY	29	
GATESHEAD	28	462
GLAMMIS	20	348
GLASGOW	23	332
GLASTONBURY	47	147
GLENCARSE	20	344
GLOSSOP	36	428
GLYNDE	50	70
GOATHLAND	29	451
GOBOWEN	31	191
GODALMING	49	91
GODSTONE	50	48
GOGAR	24	338
GOMSHALL	49	46
GOOLE	36	441
GOREBRIDGE	24	475
GORING	43	76
GORMANSTON	61	229
GOSPORT	49	96
GOWTON	28	
GOXHILL	37	433
GRAMLINGTON	25	
GRANT'S HOUSE	24	470
GRAVESEND	44	38
GREAT COATES	37	432
GREATHAM	28	457
GREENCASTLE	57	235

Station		
GREENHEAD	28	318
GREENHILL JUNCTION	23	330
GREENHITHE	44	38
GREENLOANING	20	343
GREENOCK	23	326
GRESFORD	31	195
GRETNA JUNCTION	27	326
GRISTHORPE	29	445
GROSMONT	29	451
GROVE FERRY	45	57
GT. GRIMSBY	37	433
GUILDFORD	49	46
GUISBOROUGH	28	457
GUTHRIE JUNCTION	21	349
HADBROUGH	37	
HADDINGTON	24	471
HADDISCOE	45	408
HADFIELD	36	428
HADLEIGH	44	413
HADLEY	31	282
HAILSHAM	50	71
HALSHAW	36	
HALTON	27	396
HALTWHISTLE	28	318
HAMMERTON	28	450
HAMMERWHICH	36	189
HAMPTON	43	271
HANDFORTH	31	288
HAOTON	31	
HARBURN	24	328
HARBY	29	
HARDINGHAM	38	407
HARECASTLE	31	279
HARLING ROAD	44	407
HARLOW	44	399
HARRINGTON	27	308
HARROGATE	28	446
HARROW	44	253
HARTFORD	31	285
HARTLEPOOL	28	457
HASSOCKS GATE	49	72
HASTINGDEN	31	
HASTINGS	50	51
HATFIELD	44	418
HAUGHLEY JUNCTION	45	414
HAVANT	49	78
HAVERFORDWEST	40	176
HAWICK	24	473
HAYDON BRIDGE	28	318
HAYWARDS HEATH	49	70
HAZLEHEAD	36	429
HEADCORN	50	54
HEBDEN BRIDGE	36	438
HELE	47	150
HELLIFIELD	28	395
HELMSHORE	31	435
HELPSTONE	37	379
HENLEY	43	128
HENSALL	36	441
HEREFORD	42	163
HERIOT	24	475
HERNE BAY	45	43
HERTFORD	44	398
HESSAY	28	450
HESSLE	37	442
HEST BANK	27	311
HETTON	28	
HEXHAM	28	318
HEYFORD	43	179
HEYWOOD	31	437
HIGHAM FERRERS	44	265
HIGHAM	43	40
HILGAY FEN	37	404
HILL OF DOWN & KINNEGAD	60	224
HINDLEY	31	303
HISTON	44	402
HITCHIN	44	419
HOGHTON	31	436
HOLBURN HILL	27	
HOLDERNESS	37	443
HOLME	29	441
HOLME	44	420

Station		
HOLME	37	404
HOLMES CHAPEL	31	288
HOLTON	37	432
HOLYHEAD	30	208
HOLYTOWN	23	329
HOLYWELL	31	201
HOLYWOOD	57	235
HOOTON	31	197
HORBURY ST.	36	
HORLEY	49	67
HORNBY	28	396
HORNSEY	44	417
HORSFORTH	28	455
HORSHAM	49	68
HORWICH	31	305
HOUNSLOW	44	82
HOVE	49	75
HOW MILL	27	317
HOWDEN	37	442
HOWSHAM	37	432
HOWTH	61	228
HUCKNALL TORRARD	36	381
HUDDERSFIELD	36	301
HULL	29	442
HUNGERFORD	48	130
HUNMANBY	29	445
HUNTINGDON	44	420
HUNTINGTON	29	449
HURLFORD	23	321
HUTTON	29	450
HUTTON CRANSWICK	29	444
HUYTON	31	295
ILFORD	44	409
INCHTURE	20	344
INGATESTONE	44	409
INNESHANNON	67	219
INNISKEEN	60	239
INVERESK	24	472
INVERGOWRIE	20	344
IPSWICH	45	413
IRVINE	23	322
ISLIP	43	262
IVY BRIDGE	47	156
JOHNSTONE	23	325
JUNCTION	55	228
KANTURK	63	219
KEEPHAM	37	
KEGWORTH	36	379
KEIGHLEY	28	395
KELLS	60	230
KELVEDON	44	410
KENDAL	27	312
KENYON	31	303
KETTON	37	379
KEYNSHAM	48	144
KIDWELLY	41	175
KILCOCK	60	224
KILDARE	60	212
KILKENNY	64	212
KILLARNEY	62	219
KILLINGWORTH	25	466
KILLONAN	63	215
KILLUCAN	60	224
KILMACOW	64	213
KILMALLOCK	63	217
KILMARNOCK	23	322
KILSHEELAN	64	
KILWINNING	23	322
KINBUCK	20	343
KINFAUNS	20	344
KINGHORN	24	338
KINGS LANGLEY	43	256
KINGS NORTON	42	385
KINGSBRIDGE	47	156
KINGSBURY	43	385
KINGSKETTLE	24	340
KINGSTONE	49	
KINGSTOWN	61	209
KINTBURY	48	130
KIRBY PARK	36	378
KIRK HAMMERTON	28	
KIRKBY	27	

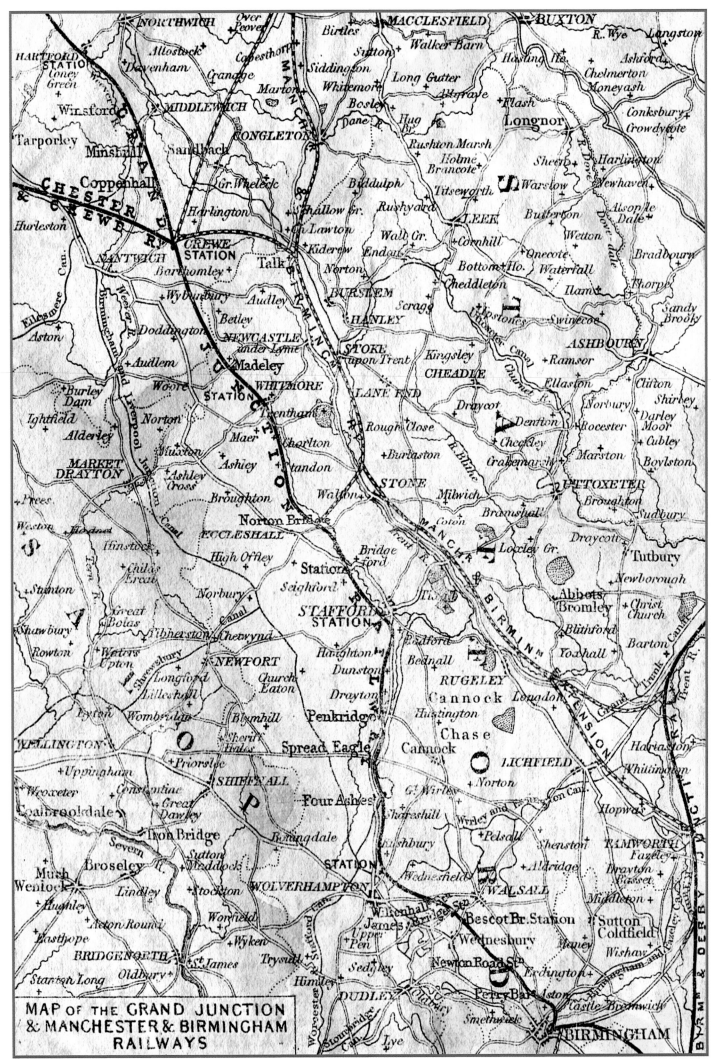

MAP OF THE GRAND JUNCTION
& MANCHESTER & BIRMINGHAM
RAILWAYS

FROM BRADSHAW'S RAILWAY COMPANION FEBRUARY 1841

KIRKBY	31		LONGFORD*	60	224	MILTON	28	317
KIRKBY	36	382	LONGFORGAN	20	344	MILLTOWN	23	336
KIRKCALDY	24	338	LONGHIRST	25	466	MINETY	42	136
KIRKHAM	29	305	LONGNIDDRY	24	471	MINSHULL VERNON	31	285
KIRKHAM	31		LONGTON	36	277	MINSTER	45	57
KIRKINTILLOCH	23	336	LOSTOCK JUNCTION	31	303	MIRFIELD	36	440
KIRKPATRICK	24	326	LOUGHBOROUGH	36	379	MOATE	60	225
KIRKSTEAD	37	423	LOUTH	37	424	MOIRA	57	377
KIRTLE BRIDGE	24	326	LOUTH	61	230	MOLD	31	200
KIRTON	37		LOWER DARWEN	31	302	MOLLINGTON	31	197
KIRTON LINDSEY	37	432	LOW GILL ST.	27	396	MONASTERVAN	60	214
KNAPTON	29		LOW ROW	28	317	MONIFIETH	21	345
KNARESBOROUGH	28	450	LOWESTOFF	45	408	MONKTON	23	322
KNOCKLONG	63		LOWDHAM	36	382	MONTROSE	21	349
KNOTANGLEY	36		LOWTHORPE	29	444	MOORE	31	285
LADYBANK	20	340	LUCAN	61	224	MOORTOWN	37	432
LAKENHEATH	44	406	LUCKER	25	467	MORETON	48	170
LAMINGTON	24	328	LUDBOROUGH	37	424	MORPETH	25	466
LANARK	23	328	LUDDENDEN FOOT	36	439	MORTIMER	49	129
LANCASTER	27	310	LUDLOW	42	170	MOSELEY	42	385
LANCING	49	76	LUFFENHAM	37	379	MOSTYN	31	201
LANGLEY	44	126	LUNCARTY	20	346	MOTHERWELL	23	329
LANGOLLEN RD.	31	194	LURGAN	57	233	MOULTON	28	422
LANGRICK	37	423	LUSK	61	229	MOUNTRATH & CASTLETOWN	64	215
LANGWORTH	37	431	LYNDHURST RD.	48	108	MOY VALLEY	60	224
LARBERT	23	330	LYNN REGIS	37	404	MUCHALLS	21	351
LARNTORTH	27		LYTHAM	31	305	MUIRKIRK	23	321
LASSIE	20		MACCLESFIELD	31	280	MULLINGAR	60	224
LAURENCEKIRK	21	350	MADELEY	31	283	MULLINAVATT	64	213
LAYTOWN	61	229	MAGDALEN GATE	37	403	MURTON	28	
LEA	36		MAGENEY	64	212	MUSSELBURGH	24	476
LEA ROAD	31		MAGHULL	31	436	MUTFORD	45	408
LEAMINGTON	43	267	MAIDENHEAD	43	127	MYTHOLMROYD	36	439
LEAMSIDE	28	461	MAIDSTONE	50	53	N. DEAN	36	
LEATON	31	191	MALAHIDE	61	228	N.TOWN ST BOSWELS	24	474
LEEBOTWOOD	42	171	MALLOW	63	217	NAFFERTON	29	444
LEEDS	36	393	MALTON	29	444	NAILSEA	48	146
LEEGATE	27	310	MANCHESTER	31	289	NANTWICH	31	284
LEEK	36	280	MANEA	44	404	NARBOROUGH	37	378
LEGBOURNE	37	424	MANGOTSFIELD	42	387	NAVAN	60	230
LEICESTER	43	376	MANNINGTREE	45	412	NEATH	41	173
LEIGH	31	303	MANSFIELD	36	382	NEEDHAM	45	414
LEIGHTON	43		MARCH	44	403	NETHERDEUGH	24	
LEITH	24	472	MARDEN	50	54	NETHERTON	25	466
LEIXLIP	60	224	MARGATE	45	59	NETHERTOWN	27	307
LENNOXTOWN	23	336	MARISHES RD	29	450	NETHERCLEUGH	24	327
LEOMINSTER	42	170	MARITON	37		NEW BELSES	24	474
LESBURY	25		MARKET RASEN	37	431	NEW CROSS	44	64
LEUCHARS JUNCTION	21	340	MARKET WEIGHTON	29	449	NEW HOLLAND	37	433
LEVISHAM	29	451	MARKINCH	24	339	NEWARK	36	426
LEWES	50	70	MARKS TEY	44	410	NEWBRIDGE	41	167
LEYSMILL	21	346	MARLANCH	20		NEWBRIDGE	60	212
LICHFIELD	36	275	MARSH BROOK	42	171	NEWBURGH	20	341
LIDLINGTON	43	260	MARSH LANE	44		NEWBURY	48	129
LIME STREET - LIVERPOOL	79	295	MARSTON GREEN	43	271	NEWCASTLE	28	463
LIMERICK	63	215	MARTON	29		NEWHAVEN	50	70
LIMERICK JUNC.	63	216	MARTON	36		NEWMARKET	44	402
LIMPET MILL	21		MARYBORO	64	215	NEWPORT	31	282
LINBY	36	382	MARYKIRK	21	350	NEWPORT	42	
LINCOLN	37	382	MARYPORT	27	309	NEWPORT	44	
LINLITHGOW	24	337	MASBRO ROTHERHAM	36	392	NEWRY	61	230
LINTON	24	471	MATLOCK BATH	36	388	NEWTON KYME	28	446
LISBURN,	57	233	MATLOCK BRIDGE	36	389	NEWTON ROAD	42	273
LIT. DURHAM	38		MAUCHLINE	23	321	NEWTOWN (NEWTON JUNCTION)	47	154
LITTLE STEEPING	37	423	MAYNOOTH	60	224	NEWTOWN STEWART	56	238
LITTLEBORO	36	438	MEIGLE	20	348	NORHAM	25	468
LITTLEHAMPTON	49	76	MELKSHAM	48	139	NORTHALLERTON	28	456
LITTLEPORT	44	404	MELLIS	45	414	NORTHAMPTON	43	263
LITTLEWORTH	37	422	MELTON	36	413	NORTH BERWICK	24	471
LIVERPOOL	31	295	MERRION	55	209	NORTHOPE	37	
LLANDILO FAWR	41		MERSTHAM	49	45	NORTON	36	
LLANELLI	41	175	MERTHYR	41	172	NORTON BR.	31	283
LLANTRISSANT	41	173	METHLEY	36	393	NORWICH	38	415
LOCHGELLY	24	339	MID CALDER	24	328	NOTTINGHAM	36	379
LOCHWINNOCH,	23	325	MIDDLE DROVE	37		NTH. KELSEY	37	432
LOCKERBIE	24	327	MIDDLESBORO	28	457	NTH. THORESBY	37	424
LOCKINGTON	29	444	MIDDLETON	28		NUNEATON	36	270
LONDON	44	15	MIDDLETON	37		OAKAMOOR	36	280
LONDONDERRY	56	238	MILDENHALL	44		OAKENGATES	31	189
LONG EATON JUNC.	36	381	MILFORD	40	176	OAKHAM	37	378
LONG PRESTON	28	395	MILLSTREET	63		OAKINGTON	44	
LONG STANTON	44	403	MILNTHORPE	27	312			

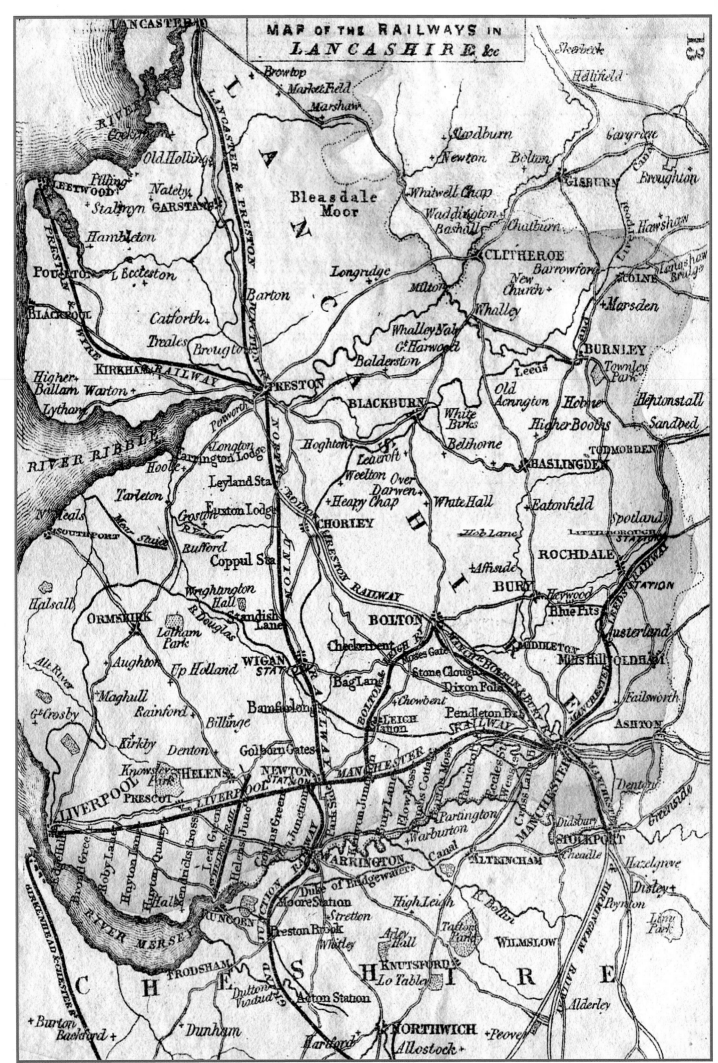

MAP OF THE RAILWAYS IN **LANCASHIRE** &c

13

ODDINGTON	43		RAHENY	55	228	SEAMER	29	445
OFFORD	44	420	RAINFORD	31	304	SEASCALE	27	307
OLD LEAKE	37	423	RAINHILL	31	295	SEATON	28	
OMAGH	56	238	RAMPSIDE	27		SELBY	36	441
ONIBURY	42	171	RAMSBOTTOM JUNCTION	31	434	SELKIRK	24	475
OOLA	63	216	RAMSGATE	45	58	SELLAFIELD	27	307
ORANMORE	59	225	RANDALSTOWN	57	237	SESSAY	28	454
ORMSKIRK	31		RANSKILL	36	426	SETTLE	28	395
ORREL	31	303	RASKELF	28	454	SHALFORD	49	46
OTTERINGTON	28	454	RATHDUFF	63		SHAP WELLS	27	315
OUGHTY BR.	36	430	RAVENGLASS	27	307	SHEFFIELD	36	430
OUNDLE	43	265	RAWCLIFFE	36	441	SHEIRE HEATH	49	
OUZEBRIDGE	37		RAYDON	44	413	SHELFORD	44	
OVER DARWEN	31	302	READING	43	128	SHENFIELD	44	
OVERTON	44	92	REARSBY	36	378	SHERBURN	28	
OXFORD	43	131	REDBRIDGE	48	93	SHERBURN	29	445
PADDOCK WOOD	50	52	REDCAR	29	457	SHIFFNALL	42	189
PALLAS	63	216	REDNAL	31	191	SHILDON	28	460
PASSAGE	63		REEDHAM	38	408	SHILTON	43	274
PANGBOURNE	43	130	REESTON	36		SHINCLIFFE	28	461
PANNAL	28	455	REIGATE	49	45	SHIPLEY	36	395
PARTON	27		RESTON	24	469	SHIPTON	29	
PATRICROFT	31	294	RETFORD	36	431	SHIREOAKS	36	431
PATTRINGTON	37	443	RHOS	31		SHORHAM	49	42
PEAKIRK	37	422	RHUABON	31		SHREWSBURY	31	189
PEEBLES	24	476	RHYL	31	201	SHRIVENHAM	43	135
PELSALL	36	189	RICHHILL	56	232	SHULFORD	49	
PEMBERTON	31	303	RICHMOND	44	82	SIBSEY	37	423
PENISTONE	36	429	RICHMOND	28	458	SILEBY	36	379
PENKRIDGE	31	274	RIDGEMONT	43	260	SILECROFT	27	307
PENMAENMAWR	30	204	RIDING MILL	28	319	SINCLAIRTOWN	24	338
PENNY	43		RILLINGTON	29	450	SION MILLS	56	238
PENRITH	27	316	RINGSTEAD	43	265	SIX MILE BOTTOM	44	401
PENSHER	28	462	RINGWOOD	48	109	SKERRIES	61	229
PENSHURST	50	49	RIPLEY	28	455	SKIPTON	28	395
PERRY BAR	42	273	RIPON	28	455	SLATEFORD	24	328
PERTH	20	343	ROADE	43	262	SLEIGHTS	29	451
PETERBORO	44	421	ROBY	31	295	SLOUGH	44	126
PICKERING	29	450	ROCESTER	36	280	SMEETH ROAD	37	403
PILLMORE JUNCTION	28	454	ROCHDALE	36	437	SNAITH	36	441
PINNER	43	255	ROMFORD	44	409	SNARESBORO	28	397
PITTINGTON	28		ROMSEY	48	94	SNELLAND	37	431
PLEASINGTON	31	436	ROSCREA & BORRIS	64	215	SOMERLAYTON	38	408
PLUCKLEY	50	54	ROSE HILL	28	317	SOUGH	31	302
PLUMPTON	27	316	ROSSETT	31	196	SOUTH GATE	44	
PLYMOUTH	47	156	ROSSINGTON	36	427	SOUTH SHIELDS	28	462
PLYMPTON	47	156	ROSTREVOR	61	231	SOUTHAMPTON	49	97
POCKLINGTON	29	449	ROWSLEY	36	389	SOUTHGATE	44	
POLEGATE JUNCTION	50	71	ROYDON,	44	399	SOUTHPORT	31	303
POLESWORTH	43	275	RUFFORD	31	436	SOUTHWAITE	27	316
PONDERS END	44	398	RUGBY	43	266	SOUTHWELL	36	382
PONTEFRACT	36	441	RUGELEY	36	276	SOUTHWICK	49	
PONTYPOOL	42	167	RUSHALL	36	189	SOUTHREY	37	423
POOLE	48	110	RUSHTON	36	280	SOWERBY BRIDGE JUNCTION	36	439
PORCHESTER	49	97	RUSWARP	29	451	SPALDING	37	422
PORTADOWN	57	231	RUTHWELL	27	319	SPEETON	29	445
PORTARLINGTON	60	214	RYBURGH	38	407	SPETCHLEY	42	
PORTHALL	56	238	RYTON	28	319	SPITAL	31	197
PORTLETHEN	21	351	SALISBURY	48	95	SPOFFORTH	28	446
PORTMARNOCK JUNC.	61	228	SALLINS	60		SPONDON	36	384
PORTOBELLO	24	472	SALTFORD	48	144	SPORLE	38	
PORT SKEWETT	42	167	SALTHILL	55	209	SPREAD EAGLE	31	274
PORTSMOUTH	49	78	SALTCOATS	23	322	SPRINGFIELD	20	340
PORT TALBOT	41	173	SALTNEY	31	196	SPRINGVALE	31	
POTMONT	24		SALWICK	31	305	SPROUSTON	24	469
POTTERS BAR	44	418	SANDBACH	31	288	ST BEES	27	307
POULTON	31		SANDWICH	45	57	ST IVES	44	403
POYNTON	31	281	SANDON	36	276	ST JOHNSON	56	
POYNTZPASS	61	231	SANDY	44	260	ST ANDREWS	21	340
PRESGWY	31		SANQUHAR	23	320	ST GERMAINS	37	
PRESTATYN	31	201	SAWBRIDGEWORTH	44	399	ST HELENS	31	294
PRESTBURY	31	281	SAWLEY	36	383	ST HELENS JUNCTION	31	295
PRESTON	31	287	SAXBY	36	378	ST LEONARDS	50	72
PRESTON BROOK	31	285	SAXILBY	36	423	ST MARGARETS	44	398
PRESTWICK	23	322	SCARBORO	29	452	ST NEOTS	44	420
PRUDHOE	28	319	SCARNING	38		STADDLETHORPE	37	442
PULFORD	31		SCAWBY	37	432	STAFFORD	31	282
PUNNAL	28		SCORTON	28	458	STAINES	49	83
PURTON	43	136	SCORTON	27	310	STALLINGBOROUGH	37	432
PYLE	41	173	SCOT. CENTRAL JUNCTION	23	337	STAMFORD BR.	29	449
PYSART	24		SCOTBY	27	317	STANDISH	31	287
RADFORD	36					STANDON BR.	31	283

Names of Railways in England and Wales as numbered on page 68						
	Miles	Amt. of share			Miles	Amt. of share
1. Birmingham & Derby Junction	38	£100	21. Manchester and Birmingham		45	£70
2. Birmingham & Gloucester ..	52	100	21. Manchester and Birmingham Ex		-	70
3. Birmingham, Bristol & Thames Junction	3	20	22. Manchester and Leeds		60	100
4. Bolton and Leigh			23. Manchester, Bolton & Bury ..		10	100
4. Kenyon and Leigh	10	100	24. Maryport and Carlisle		28	50
5. Bristol and Exeter	76	100	25. Midland Counties		57	100
6. Bolton and Preston	14	50	26. Newcastle and Carlisle		61	100
7. Chester and Birkenhead ..	15	50	27. Newcastle and North Sheilds		$6\frac{3}{4}$	50
7. Chester and Crewe	18	50	28. North Midland		72	100
8. Cromford and High Peak ..	$32\frac{3}{4}$	-	29. North Union		22	75
9. Croydon	10	-	30. Northern and Eastern		52	100
10. Eastern Counties	126	25	31. St. Helen's and Runcorn Gap		8	100
11. Grand Junction	97	-	32. Sheffield and Manchester ..		40	100
12. Great North England	74	100	33. Sheffield and Rothergam ..		6	25
13. Great Western	17	100	34. Stockton and Darlington ..		25	100
14. Hull and Selby	30	50	35. York and North Midland ..		23	50
15. Lancaster and Preston Junction	20	50	36. South Eastern and Dover ..		67	50
16. Leeds and Selby	20	100	37. Canterbury and Whitstable ..		6	50
17. Leicester and Swannington ..	16	50	38. Greenwich		4	20
18. Liverpool and Manchester ..	31	100	39. Preston and Wyre		19	50
19. London and Birmingham ..	112	100	40. Taff Vale		-	-
20. London and Southampton ..	76	-	41. Manchester and Bolton Extension		-	-
			42. London and Brighton		46	50

EDGE HILL RAILWAY STATION, LIVERPOOL - 1838

Station		
STANLEY	20	346
STANSTEAD	44	399
STANTHORPE	28	
STAPLEHURN	50	
STAPLEHURST	50	54
STARCROSS	47	
STAVELEY	27	312
STAVELEY	36	392
STAYLEY BRIDGE	36	300
STETCHFORD	42	271
STEVENAGE	44	418
STEVENTON	43	135
STIRLING	23	330
STIXWOULD	37	423
STOCKBRIDGE	36	93
STOCKPORT	31	288
STOCKSFIELD	28	319
STOCKTON	29	
STOCKTON	28	456
STOKE WORKS	42	386
STONE	36	276
STONECLOUGH	36	302
STONEHAVEN	21	350
STONEHOUSE	42	137
STOW	24	
STOW	37	
STOW MARKET	45	414
STRABANE	56	238
STRAFFAN	61	
STRATFORD	43	397
STRATRY	44	
STREAMSTOWN	60	225
STRENSALL	29	
STRETTON	36	274
STRETTON	43	
STROOD	44	40
STROUD	42	137
STUBBINS	31	434
STURRY	45	57
STURTON	36	432
SUDBURY	36	278
SUDBURY	44	411
SUMMERSEAT	31	434
SUNDERLAND	28	462
SURFLEET	37	422
SUTTON	36	382
SUTTON	31	197
SUTTON	49	66
SWAINSTHORP	38	415
SWANSEA	41	174
SWAVESEY	44	403
SWINDERBY	37	382
SWINDON JUNCTION	42	136
SYMINGTON	24	328
SYSTON	36	378
TADCASTER	28	446
TAMWORTH	36	275
TANDERAGEE AND GUILFORD	57	231
TATTENHALL	31	284
TATTERSHALL	37	423
TAUNTON	47	148
TEBAY	27	315
TEIGNMOUTH	47	154
TEMPLEMORE	63	216
TETBURY ROAD	42	136
THANKERTON	24	328
THRAPSTON	43	265
THATCHAM	49	129
THEALE	49	129
THETFORD	44	406
THIRSK	28	454
THOMASTOWN	64	213
THORNHILL	23	320
THORNTON	24	339
THORNTON ABBEY	37	433
THORP ARCH	28	446
THORPE	43	382
THURGARTON	36	382
THURLES	63	216
THURSTON	44	402
TIPPERARY	63	215
TIVERTON JUNCTION	47	149

Station		
TIVETSHALL	45	414
TOLLERTON	28	454
TOPCLIFFE	28	456
TORQUAY	47	154
TOTNESS	47	156
TRAMORE	64	214
TRANENT	24	472
TRIMDON	28	461
TRING	43	257
TROON	23	322
TROOPERS LANE	57	235
TROWBRIDGE	48	139
TROWSE	38	408
TUNBRIDGE	50	49
TUTBURY	36	278
TWERTON	48	144
TWYFORD	43	128
TY CROES	30	208
TYRIE HEAD	24	
UFFINGTON	37	379
ULCEBY J.	37	432
ULLESTHORP	43	376
ULVERSTON	27	306
UPHOLLAND	31	303
UPTON & BRINNY	67	219
UPTON MAGNA	31	189
USSELBY	37	432
UTTOXETER JUNC	36	277
VALLEY	30	208
VELVET HALL	25	
VICTORIA BRIDGE	56	238
WADBOROUGH	42	386
WADSLEY BR.	36	430
WALCOT	31	189
WALLINGFORD	43	130
WALSALL	36	188
WALSOKEN	37	
WALTHAM	37	398
WALTHAM	44	398
WALTON	49	89
WAMPHRAY	24	327
WANSFORD	43	265
WANTAGE	43	135
WARE	44	398
WAREHAM	48	110
WARKWORTH	25	466
WARMINSTER	42	140
WARRENPOINT	61	231
WARRINGTON	31	285
WASHINGBORO	37	423
WATER LANE	44	
WATER ORTON	42	385
WATERBEACH	44	403
WATERFALL	63	219
WATERFORD	64	213
WATERINGBURY	50	52
WATERLOO	31	304
WATFORD	43	255
WATH	28	393
WATTINGTON	37	
WAVERTON	31	284
WEEDON	43	266
WEETON	28	455
WELLINGBORO	43	265
WELLINGTON	31	282
WELLINGTON	47	149
WELWYN	44	418
WENDLING	38	406
WENNINGTON	28	396
WEST DRAYTON	44	126
WEST HAM & PEVENSEY	50	71
WESTBURY	42	140
WESTENHANGER	50	60
WESTHOUGHTON	38	303
WESTON	36	276
WETHERALL	27	317
WETHERBY	28	446
WEXFORD	64	228
WEYBRIDGE	49	89
WHIFFLET	23	329
WHISENDINE	37	378
WHITACRE J.	43	385

Station		
WHITBY	29	451
WHITCHURCH	49	284
WHITEABBEY	57	235
WHITEHAVEN	27	307
WHITLEY BR.	36	441
WHITMORE	31	283
WHITTINGTON	31	191
WHITTLESFORD	44	399
WICKENBY	37	431
WICKHAM MARKET J	44	413
WICKLOW	65	227
WICKWAR	42	387
WIDDRINGTON	25	466
WIGAN	31	286
WIGSTON	43	375
WIGTON	27	310
WILLENHALL	42	273
WILLINGTON	36	385
WILLOUGHBY	37	424
WILNECOTE & FAZELEY	43	385
WITHERNSEA	37	443
WIMBLINGTON	44	403
WIMSLOW	31	288
WINDERMERE	27	312
WINCHBURGH	24	337
WINCHESTER	49	93
WINCHFIELD	49	92
WINDSOR	43	83
WINGATE	28	461
WINGFIELD	36	391
WINSFORD	31	285
WISBEACH	37	403
WITHAM	44	410
WITHERNSEA	37	443
WITTON JUNCTION	28	460
WOBURN SANDS	43	260
WOKING	49	90
WOKINGHAM	49	47
WOLVERHAMPTON	42	180
WOLVERTON	43	262
WOMERSLEY	36	428
WOODHEAD	36	429
WOODHOUSE MILL	36	392
WOODLAWN	59	
WOODLESFORD	36	393
WOODSIDE	20	348
WOODSTOCK ROAD	43	179
WOOFERTON	42	170
WOOL	48	111
WOOLHAMPTON	49	129
WOOLWICH	44	37
WOOTON BASSET	42	139
WORKINGTON	27	308
WORKSOP	36	431
WORMALD GREEN	28	455
WORCESTER	42	183
WORTHING	49	76
WORTLEY	36	302
WRAY	28	
WRAYSBURY	43	83
WREXHAM	31	195
WYCOMBE	43	127
WYE	50	55
WYLAM	28	319
WYMONDHAM	44	407
YALDING	50	52
YAPTON	49	
YARM	28	456
YARMOUTH	38	408
YATE	42	387
YATTON	47	146
YAXHAM	38	407
YEOVIL	48	148
YORK	29	447

PICTURE CREDITS

Railway Maps and British Town Plans

Mapseeker Archive Publishing Ltd
www.mapseeker.co.uk
www.oldmapsandimages.co.uk

Pictorial images Views, Vistas and other Artefacts.

Mapseeker Archive Publishing Ltd
With special thanks to the following in the sourcing of antique original resources art
worked for this atlas publication
Berian Williams Antique Maps and prints
www.antique-prints-maps.co.uk
Steve Bartrick Maps and prints
www.antiqueprints.com
Ash Rare Books
www.ashrare.com
Jonathon Potter Antique Maps Ltd
www.jpmaps.co.uk
Arthur Hook Old Maps and Books
www.hooksbooks.co.uk

All of the John Tallis Town Plans featured in this atlas are available as photographic
prints and in a range of other products on www.mapseeker.co.uk and www.
oldmapsandimages.co.uk

DEDICATION TO GEORGE BRADSHAW

George Bradshaw's enduring legacy to the nation – one created through his many railway maps - is a compelling insight into the nature of railway travel at the height of Victorian eminence. Ten years before he produced the first iconic railway map in 1839, entitled "Map and Sections of the Railways of Great Britain", he had already built up a considerable reputation for his large canal maps of Great Britain, the first maps of inland navigation. However, it was the publication of "Bradshaw's Railway Companion," an indispensable travel guide which contained train timetables, maps and vivid descriptions of towns and cities, that marked the beginnings of world acclaim. December 1841 saw the title of this regular and innovative publication change to "Bradshaw's Guide" which would become forever synonymous with rail travel. His business partnership with William Blacklock forged a massive company that would gain international recognition, one that prospered long after George Bradshaw's early passing in 1853 and well into the 20th century. It is fitting that for someone who was on the forefront of innovation that the latest digital technology allows the fame of George Bradshaw to continue into the 21st century – and that the instrumental resources required for that to happen would be the rare surviving publications his company produced back in mid Victorian times.

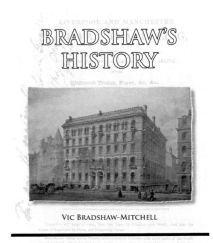

BRADSHAW'S GUIDE: The 1866 Handbook
Reprinted ISBN 9781908174055

BRADSHAW'S HISTORY: The compelling story of the
famous George Bradshaw ISBN 9781908174185

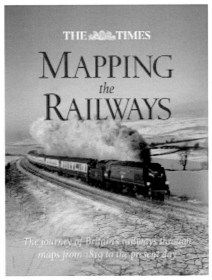

THE TIMES MAPPING
THE RAILWAYS: The
journey of Britain's
railways through maps
from 1819 to the present
day ISBN 9780007435999

BRADSHAWS'S
RAILWAY MAP 1839:
Wall map supplied in
a tube showing the
Railways of Great
Britain along with
gradient profiles: ISBN
9880007480289

BRADSHAW'S
RAILWAY MAP OF
GREAT BRITAIN
AND IRELAND 1852:
Laminated wall map
supplied in a tube
showing all the stations:
ISBN 9781844917921

OSBORNES MAP
OF THE GRAND
JUNCTION
RAILWAY 1837:
Laminated wall map
supplied in a tube
showing the detailed
route and stations of
the Grand Junction
Railway: ISBN
9781844917938